Castle Rock Kitchen transports you to Stephen King's Castle Rock multiverse—a darker, more gothic version of the Maine you are familiar with—through eighty immersive recipes written from the perspective of Mrs. Garraty, a character first introduced in *The Long Walk* and a lifelong resident of King's Maine. Ranging from down-home breakfasts to luscious desserts (and every course in between), these modern, mouthwatering dishes are inspired by meals and gatherings from more than forty novels and stories set in Castle Rock, Derry, and other King-created towns.

Theresa Carle-Sanders, professional chef and author of the *Outlander Kitchen* cookbooks, feeds hunger both real and fictional with classic, satisfying dishes such as Pancakes with the Toziers (*It*), One-Handed Frittata (*Under the Dome*), Whopper Spareribs (*The Tommyknockers*), Lobster Pickin's (*11/22/63*), Wild Mushroom Hand Pies (*Bag of Bones*), Dolores's Oven Risotto (*Dolores Claiborne*), Blueberry Cheesecake Pie ("The Body"), and Homemade Root Beer (*Carrie*). With a foreword written by Stephen King and story excerpts that connect the recipes to the books that inspired them, *Castle Rock Kitchen* delivers frightfully good food and drink.

CASTLE ROCK KITCHEN

Wicked Good Recipes

FROM THE WORLD OF Stephen King

CASTLE ROCK KITCHEN

Theresa Carle-Sanders

FOREWORD BY STEPHEN KING

PHOTOGRAPHS BY JENNY BRAVO

TEN SPEED PRESS
California | New York

To my dad, Ralph.
You taught me the pleasures of eating fresh and local,
decades before I heard it from anyone else.
We still cook breakfast together every Sunday in my dreams.

CONTENTS

FOREWORD

By Stephen King

I was born in Maine, grew up in Maine, and expect to be buried in Maine. Before that happens, I'll continue to eat in Maine, and many of the things I've eaten are presented (under different names in most cases) in this lovely little cookbook.

When people think of Maine cuisine, they tend to think first of clams and lobster. Never cared for clams myself; they always looked to me like snot in a shell. Lobster is tasty, but I ate too much of it as a kid. My mom was on a perpetual budget, and she'd buy day-old (or *two*-day-old) lobster at the IGA in Lisbon Falls. Some of those bugs were still moving, but not that many. She made lobster rolls, and there was often a pot of lobster stew simmering on the stove. She'd hide it in the oven if someone came visiting because, in those days, lobster stew was "poor food."

When I think of Maine cuisine, I think of red hot dogs in spongy Nissen rolls, slow-baked beans (with a big chunk of pork fat thrown in), steamed fresh peas with bacon, whoopie pies, plus macaroni and cheese (often with lobster bits, if there were some left over). I think of creamed salt cod on mashed potatoes—a favorite of my toothless grandfather—and haddock baked in milk, which was the only fish my brother would eat. I hated it; to this day I can see those fishy fillets floating in boiled milk with little tendrils of butter floating around in the pan. Ugh.

As the twig is bent the bough is shaped, so they say, and my tastes have remained simple and unrefined. I like nothing better than a couple of blueberry pancakes for breakfast, floating in maple syrup. (Folks think of Vermont when they think of maple syrup, but the Maine variety is just as good.) There's nothing like a chunk of fried fish with vinegar for lunch, and a New England boiled dinner for supper—corned beef, cabbage, potatoes, and carrots. ("You must *zimmer* very *zlowly*," my mother liked to say.) Add some strawberry shortcake (Bisquick biscuits, please) for dessert, and you've got some mighty good eatin'.

We like to see you up here in Vacationland, always glad to fix you up with all the crabmeat salad and lobster rolls you can eat (extra points if you ask for *lobstah*), but if you can't come, you can always browse the recipes in this book, which are drawn from some of my stories and novels. If you're in a campfire frame of mind, you might finish off with s'mores, and if you're in your cabin up St. John's Valley way (or just imagining it), you could start your day of huntin', trappin', and fishin' with a bowl of Muddy Buddy.

May I close with a Maine food joke?

Loggers are out in the woods, y'see, and they need someone to do the cooking. Pete Bouchard gets the call, because he's the smallest—if he turned sideways he'd disappear, don'tcha know. Not given much in the way of choice, Pete says, "I'll cook until someone says they don't like it. Then that person gets the apron."

Well, they all agree to that, but a logging crew is in the woods all winter, and Pete gets damn tired of doing the cooking. He starts boiling the potatoes to mush, burning the venison steaks to cinders, leaving bird shot in the birds so the loggers have to spit 'em out, serves cakes so hard they'd break a tooth. Yet everyone in the crew keeps saying *It's good, Petie, it's good, it's really good.*

Finally, in desperation, Pete goes out in the woods one day and picks up a big bag of fresh moose droppings. He bakes it in a pie and covers it with whipped cream (I don't know where he got cream in the deep woods either, so don't ask). That night he serves it out. Severin Belliveau takes a great big bite and says, "God-*damn*! This is moose-shit pie! *But it's good! It's good!*"

There are no recipes for moose-shit pie in this book, but you'll find the taste of Castle Rock, Maine, in every one. Even if you don't … imagine. It's what I do.

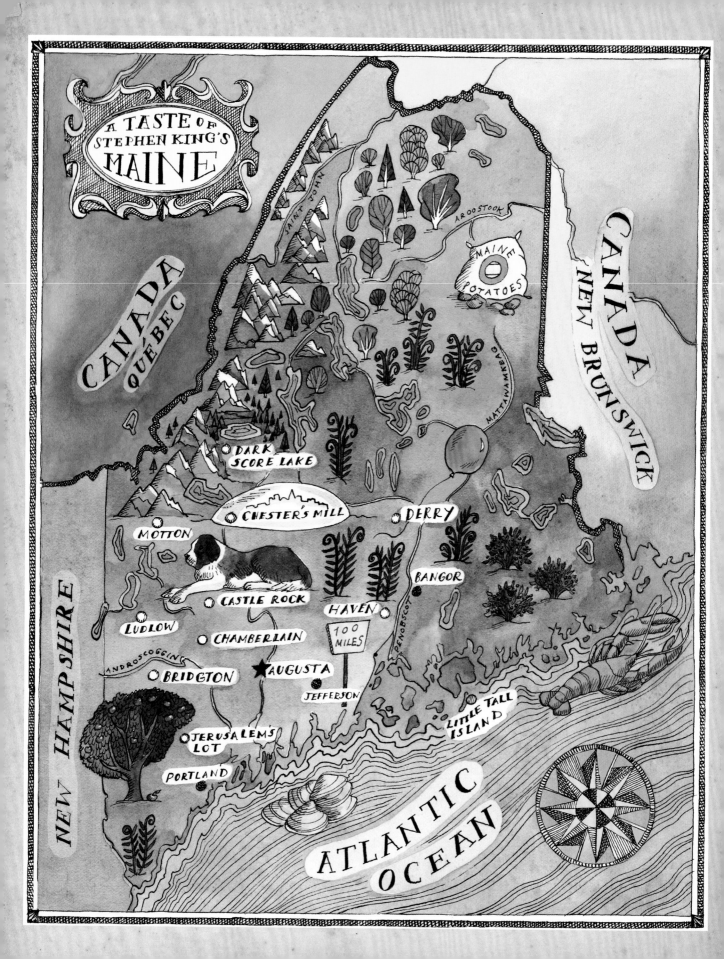

INTRODUCTION

Stephen King's Maine is not the one you know. The border between realities has worn thin in places, and the horrors that dwell on the other side cross over—sometimes unseen, other times with devastating results. The following recipes come from *that* Maine, so it's fitting to have someone who lives there share them with you.

You may have met Mrs. Garraty before, at the beginning of the first novel Stephen King ever wrote: *The Long Walk*. In the story, set in a not-so-distant dystopian future, one hundred young men volunteer to undergo an annual Walk that starts on the Maine–New Brunswick border and proceeds south until just one Walker is left standing.

Ray Garraty is the home-state favorite, and a bona fide Maine's Own, his family having lived there for generations. His mother, Mrs. Garraty, although a minor character, has an authoritative voice when it comes to Maine home cooking; she has access to family and regional recipes passed down for decades, including her Hermits for the Road (page 187), which she gives to Ray just before he starts the Walk. She also has insights into the other Stephen King stories set in Maine, having heard the tales from Castle Rock, Derry, and Chester's Mill, to name just three of King's fictional towns.

Other characters have influenced Mrs. Garraty's narrative voice: Dolores Claiborne, inspired by Nellie King, the author's own mother; Stella Flanders from "The Reach," the most Maine character he ever wrote; the moms from *It*; and the housewives from *Needful Things*. They've all come together to create a cookbook homage to the great state of Maine and its storytelling King.

Join Mrs. G. and me in our Castle Rock Kitchen to explore Stephen King's Maine multiverse and eighty recipes, from the mouthwatering to the macabre, inspired by his stories. Frighteningly delicious adventures await!

MY CASTLE ROCK KITCHEN

```
"I made these. You can take them, can't you? They're not too heavy,
are they?" She thrust a foil-wrapped package of cookies at him.

"Yeah." He took them and then clutched her awkwardly, trying to give
her what she needed to have. He kissed her cheek. Her skin was like
old silk. For a moment he could have cried himself. Then he thought
of the smiling, mustachioed face of the Major and stepped back,
stuffing the cookies into the pocket of his fatigue jacket.

"G'bye, Mom."

"Goodbye, Ray. Be a good boy."
```

———————

THE LONG WALK

I was born in Maine, and here I'll die—wouldn't leave even if I had the will to defy the Major, the beast who lured away my last boy and forever changed him—who wouldn't be changed, after walking all those days at death's doorstep with ninety-nine others and seeing them Ticketed away, one by one?

If I could go back, I would have leaned harder on Ray to use the April 31st backout. I don't know why I didn't. I kid myself, saying he never would have quit anyway, and maybe I'm right, but I'll never know; I froze. His brother was dead, his father gone, and I stayed silent until it was too late, even as the Major stole him from me.

So here I remain, content that the Prize Ray earned will keep us in comfort. Others scrape and scrounge for every last morsel while I cook from the recipes passed down to me by my mother and grandmothers, never mind the cost. The food of Maine's past keeps us warm and fed, despite the never-ending uncertainty of our future. Some of the recipes in this collection are from family, others are from women's associations and church cookbooks, and a few are inspired by the maven of traditional Down East cooking, Marjorie Standish. Mama said Grandma clipped her column from the *Portland Sunday Telegram* every week.

If you weren't born here, then you're from away. I don't make the rules, that's just how things are. The first European settlers blended their own familiar fare from home with indigenous foods such as lobster, clams, turkey, corn, squash, cranberries, blueberries, and maple syrup. Hundreds of years later, Maine traditions include baked beans, brown bread, lobster stew, fish chowder, clam rolls, and winter-squash doughnuts.

Years ago, it seemed like every family in Maine, and in the rest of New England, had their own way with a Sunday Boiled Dinner (page 54). I haven't seen a gray, freshly corned brisket since before Ray was born—most people prefer the pink of nitrates these days—but I still make a boiled dinner at least once a month, even if canned corned beef is all I can get.

Other recipes I wrote down from those old-timers still in their right enough mind to remember how food used to taste, like Killer Mac and Cheese (page 49) and the crispy-skinned chicken thighs from the Blue Plate Special (page 65)—an old friend's twist on the gravy-smothered open-faced turkey sandwiches served up in family-run diners along US 1—and a great way to use up leftover Potato Stuffing (page 166).

Another friend who had a big influence on me in the kitchen was the mother of my best friend, Amelia. Her mom, my Auntie Mae, came with her family from China. Her family stayed in Portland and opened a Chinese American restaurant, but Mae fell in love with a boy from Pownal, got pregnant, and their daughter was my best friend all through school.

I think it's because of Mae that I grew so open to talking to strangers. She broadened my world to more than just Chinese food, despite the fact I've never been farther than the islands off Freeport. I get farther listening to the stories from the people come here to watch the boys Walk than I'll ever get on my own two feet. Ayuh, my lot has been cast, and it's Maine for me, until the end.

That doesn't mean there aren't some hazards to look out for near to home, especially in the kitchen. I've spent most of my life next to the stove with a knife in my hand and had nothing more than minor burns and cuts, I'm proud to say.

Tips

Here's a short list of some of what I've learned about staying safe while getting the work done quick as you can.

Read the recipe through before you go shopping, and then at least once more before you start. Prepare the ingredients as instructed on the list before you begin, and everything will go smoothly. You might even enjoy yourself.

Take a knife-skills course at a local culinary school or kitchenware store. Two or three hours learning how to hold your knife, basic technique and safety, as well as how to keep your knives sharp will go a long way to keeping all your fingers on both hands. There you will learn my favorite, but relatively unknown, knife cut, the julienne. To julienne, cut the ingredient into short thin strips, like matchsticks. In particular, I prefer to julienne onions. The uniform slivers of a julienned onion cook more evenly than the random-size rings from a sliced one. You can also find instructional videos online.

Use all your senses when you're cooking and baking, not just taste. Watch the dough to make sure it doesn't overproof; smell the garlic bloom in the hot pan and take it off the heat before it burns and turns bitter. Listen to the change in the sound of the oil as the fish batter crisps; learn to test the doneness of meat with the touch of your hand, rather than relying on a thermometer.

Common Phrases

I use these phrases repeatedly throughout the recipes that follow.

Taste and season with salt and pepper—always taste before you season, and remember to season for everyone at the table, not just yourself—keep that in mind when you're cooking with spices and chiles, too, like in Holy Frijole Enchiladas (page 147).

Bring a large pot of generously salted water to a boil—a "large pot" means at least 1 gallon of water, and "generous" salting requires 2 tablespoons of kosher salt; the food absorbs the salt as it cooks, seasoning it from the inside out.

Pour into a shallow metal bowl or plate, set on top of a wire rack or trivet, and stir occasionally to cool quickly—metal dissipates heat quickly; use this method to cool down such things as sautéed vegetables or lemon curd without putting hot, steaming plates in the refrigerator.

Prepare an ice bath by filling a large bowl (or bucket) with ice and cold water—use it to cool blanched items, like fiddleheads and lobsters, or float a bowl full of steaming chicken stock on top of the ice bath and stir occasionally to cool.

Cover the bowl with a clean dish towel and then a plate—I cover all my rising dough like this, and often store leftovers in the fridge the same way.

Set the bowl in a warm, draft-free place to rise—draft-free places in your kitchen include the warming drawer under your oven, on the stove top with the overhead light on, and inside the oven with the interior light on.

Keep watch on the oil as you proceed—efficiency in the kitchen is important, but safety always comes first. Set the deep-fry oil over medium heat so it can warm while you work, but never turn your back on a pot of hot oil. Remember to check it every few minutes.

NOTE

No thermometer? Check the temperature of the oil by sticking the end of a wooden spoon or chopstick into the oil. When lots of bubbles form around the wood and float to the surface, your oil is ready for frying. If it is bubbling very vigorously, the oil is too hot; take it off the heat to cool for a few minutes and then check the temperature again.

Pantry Notes

Here's a list of some of my pantry staples and their uses.

Allen's Coffee Brandy—Allen's is the most popular liquor in the state of Maine. At 30% ABV, it's a half again as strong as Kahlua, a coffee liqueur. You can use another brand of coffee brandy or coffee liqueur if you can't find Allen's, though trust me when I say it just won't be the same.

Bakewell Cream—a raising agent invented in Maine in WWII as a response to a shortage of cream of tartar and baking powder, it's been a statewide pantry staple ever since. For the lightest and fluffiest baked goods, combine two parts Bakewell Cream with one part baking soda as a replacement for baking powder in most recipes. Specific amounts are given in a recipe's Note when the calculations get tricky.

Beans—Mainers prefer larger cooking beans such as Marfax, yellow eye, or kidney, while our southern New England neighbors tend to use the smaller navy or great northern beans. The choice is up to you.

Bell's Seasoning—this poultry seasoning has been irreplaceable in New England kitchens since 1867. A blend of ground rosemary, oregano, sage, ginger, marjoram, thyme, and pepper, it is salt-, gluten-, additive-, and preservative-free. You can use another poultry seasoning, but it won't taste as good.

Butter—I use salted and unsalted butter interchangeably at home. Unless I specify one or the other in a recipe, use what you have on hand.

Buttermilk—I'm never without at least a pint in the fridge. I've heard that in some places these days, buttermilk can be hard to find. Although not the real thing, clabbered milk works in a pinch: combine 1 cup milk and 1 tablespoon fresh lemon juice or vinegar and let stand at room temperature for 15 minutes until thickened and curdled.

Eggs—I always use large.

Flour—all-purpose flour is just that. I use it for everything from sandwich bread to whoopie pies. I also keep 00 durum flour on hand for my pizza and pasta doughs. It's higher in protein, with a finer grind than all-purpose, resulting in a baby-bottom soft dough that transforms into pastas and pizza crusts with just the right amount of bite.

Milk—I always use whole.

Oil—sunflower and grapeseed are good choices for neutral-tasting, everyday vegetable oils. They're perfectly good for deep-frying, but if I have peanut oil on hand, I prefer to use it for its light taste. When a recipe calls for olive oil, I use extra-virgin.

Salt—kosher salt is standard in my kitchen, except for a few recipes where it is too coarse; those call for table salt or fine sea salt.

Spices—pre-ground spices stale quickly. Paprika, cayenne, and ground pepper have an especially short shelf life. Use them within 6 months of opening.

White vermouth—I always have a bottle of it in the pantry. It's my secret, shelf-stable substitute for white wine in cooking.

Equipment

I don't use a lot of special equipment in my kitchen, but there are a few tools I can't do without. If you find yourself without something on the following list, ask your neighbors if they have one you can borrow. And be sure to gift them back with some of what you make.

Bench scrapers—a metal scraper with a straight edge to scrape the counter and cut dough, and a silicone, curved-edge scraper to maneuver and toss dough in the bowl.

Chef's knife—buy the best one you can afford; it helps to pick up and hold several before buying to find the one that best fits your hand.

Food processor—a small, inexpensive food processor for making dressings, sauces, and marinades is very handy. Large food processors often come with a small bowl and a smaller blade that you can set inside the big one.

Handheld mixer—used to beat cake batters and cookie doughs.

Immersion blender—a stick-style blender used to puree soups and sauces in the pan or a bowl. Quicker to use and clean up than a food processor or countertop blender.

Instant-read thermometer—take the temperatures of roasting meat, candy in the making, and oil for deep-frying.

Microplane—the modern, kitchen version of the rasp my daddy had in his workshop. Grate zest off the surface of a lemon, make a quick paste of garlic and/or ginger (skin and all), and grate a light cloud of Parmesan over pasta.

Pasta roller—you *can* roll out pasta with a rolling pin, but it's a lot of work.

Breakfast

For the first meal of the day, one that's supposed to get you up and running, there's not many people left who give it the importance we used to. Toaster pastries, cereal in cardboard boxes, and fast food from bags may look nutritious on paper with all those enriched vitamins, but none of it fuels a day of hard work like the real breakfasts I remember from when I was a girl.

Real food like fruit. There's wild blueberries in my oatmeal and cranberries in my French toast, both grown in plenty along the coast in the tidal flats. In the south of the state, thousands of acres are devoted to apples; Maine still grows the sweetest eating and best cooking apples, as we have for well over a hundred years.

No one ever passes up one of the apple-cinnamon rolls my dad's mom made for a treat every Sunday in the winter. She stored the apples in the root cellar, and that's where she left the rolls to rest in the morning, until we were home from church. These days, I let my dough rest in the fridge, and my oven cooks more evenly than her old woodstove ever did, but the sweet, gooey, apple-cinnamon filling still tastes just like Grannie made.

The best homegrown breakfasts are sweetened with Maine maple syrup. It's expensive now, even in-state, but avoid the cheap fake stuff and treat yourself to the real thing. Drizzle it on oatmeal or pancakes, bake some straight into an overnight French toast casserole, or add a little to homemade pork sausage to lend a bit of sweetness to your sausage on cheese biscuits.

When Ray was little, he loved to watch a Dutch baby pancake puff up through the glass in the oven door. Out of the oven, it collapses back into the pan, leaving a tender, eggy pancake the size of a French crêpe—the perfect base for banana-pecan compote—and large enough to share.

I know most of these recipes won't come together quick enough for some of you living life in the fast lane, but a four-egg omelet is some of the most real food there is, whether it's for breakfast, dinner, or supper—and eggs are always fast. No dainty, colorless omelets from gay Paree for this Mainer. This is an American omelet, golden brown on the bottom, and filled with whatever you please, not necessarily just cheese and mushrooms.

That's the kind of breakfast I'm talking about. Eat up—you never know what the day will bring.

That morning he had awakened next to his wife, and had eaten breakfast across from his son. They talked about stuff, like people do. We never know. Any day could be the day we go down, and we never know.

REVIVAL

On March 12th, 1975, the cell doors in Cellblock 5 opened at 6:30 a.m., as they do every morning around here except Sunday. And as they do every day except Sunday, the inmates of those cells stepped forward into the corridor and formed two lines as the cell doors slammed shut behind them. They walked up to the main cellblock gate, where they were counted off by two guards before being sent on down to the cafeteria for a breakfast of oatmeal, scrambled eggs, and fatty bacon.

"RITA HAYWORTH AND SHAWSHANK REDEMPTION"

Life-Sentence Oatmeal

Makes 4 servings

Blueberries and maple syrup combine with steel-cut oats and creamy coconut milk for a sweet, rib-sticking bowl of oatmeal that's much tastier than the slop they served to Andy, Red, and the rest of the boys in Shawshank State Prison.

Wild blueberries are sweeter and more flavorful than their cultivated cousins. That said, using what you have on hand is one of the first rules in my kitchen.

One 13.5-ounce can unsweetened low-fat coconut milk

1 cup water

2 tablespoons maple syrup, plus more for serving

¼ teaspoon kosher salt

1 cup quick-cooking steel-cut oats

½ teaspoon vanilla extract

1 cup fresh or frozen wild blueberries, plus more for serving

Toasted coconut flakes for serving

In a medium saucepan over medium-high heat, combine the coconut milk, water, maple syrup, and salt and bring to a low boil. Slowly pour in the oats and, stirring continuously, bring back to a boil. Turn the heat to medium-low and simmer, stirring occasionally, until the oats are cooked, 5 to 7 minutes.

Remove the pan from the heat, stir in the vanilla and blueberries, cover, and let sit for 5 minutes.

Serve the oatmeal immediately, passing more maple syrup, fresh blueberries, and coconut flakes at the table.

```
"When the Clark twins do it all, you give them two dollars each!"

"That's true," Went admitted. "But as far as I know, they don't want
to go to the movies tomorrow. Or if they do, they must have funds
sufficient to the occasion, because they haven't popped by to check
the state of the herbiage surrounding our domicile lately. . . .
That pressure you feel in your midsection may be the five pancakes and
two eggs you ate for breakfast, Richie, or it may just be the barrel
I have you over. Wot-wot?"
```

—

IT

Pancakes with the Toziers

Makes 4 servings

I'm sure Mrs. Tozier fed her son, Richie, well, which is more than I can say for most of those other parents in Derry. 'Course, that's nothing compared to the dozens of missing children so quickly forgotten. Fearful stories of something beneath the streets, haunting the sewers.

This banana–browned butter Dutch baby pancake was my Ray's favorite breakfast as a kid. When I sent him out fishing or foraging in the afternoon after school, I'd roll up a cold one of these with the banana-pecan compote or some jam, then slice it into pinwheels for easy snacking.

BROWNED BUTTER
¼ cup butter

3 eggs
¾ cup milk
1 ripe large banana
2 tablespoons light brown sugar
½ teaspoon kosher salt
¾ cup all-purpose flour
Banana-Pecan Compote (recipe follows)
or maple syrup (optional) for serving

Position an oven rack on the lower-middle rung and heat the oven to 425°F.

To make the browned butter: In a 9- or 10-inch cast-iron or other ovenproof skillet over medium-high heat, melt the butter. Turn the heat to medium and brown the butter, stirring occasionally; at the start, the butter will steam and spit as the water in it evaporates. Next, the color will deepen as white foam appears on the surface and milk solids float near the bottom of the pan. Watch the butter closely and stir continuously as the color deepens and a nutty aroma fills the air.

CONTINUED

When the milk solids are golden brown, 3 to 6 minutes, remove from the heat, swirl the butter to coat the pan, and pour the browned butter into a small bowl. Reserve for the compote or to serve.

In a blender, combine the eggs, milk, banana, brown sugar, and salt. Add the flour on top and blend on high speed until pale and smooth, about 1 minute. Pour the batter into the hot pan and bake until the Dutch baby is puffed and the edges are golden, 15 to 20 minutes. Transfer the skillet to a wire rack to cool for 2 to 3 minutes.

Slice the Dutch baby into wedges and serve with the compote or the remaining browned butter and maple syrup.

Banana-Pecan Compote

Makes about 2 cups

Serve with a Dutch baby, pancakes, waffles, or ice cream.

½ cup chopped pecans

3 tablespoons browned butter (see page 13)

1 ripe large banana, sliced lengthwise and cut into ½-inch slices

¼ cup unpacked light brown sugar

¼ teaspoon kosher salt

In a medium saucepan over medium heat, toast the pecans until light golden and aromatic, 3 to 5 minutes. Stir in the browned butter, banana, brown sugar, and salt and cook, stirring occasionally, until the mixture is bubbling and the banana starts to break down, 4 to 5 minutes. Remove from the heat.

Transfer to an airtight container and store in the refrigerator for up to 3 days. Warm in the microwave before serving.

The real thing was the thought of food.

Breakfasts, for instance, take breakfasts: two eggs fried in butter, over easy if you don't mind, waiter. French toast. Big glasses of fresh-squeezed orange juice so cold that moisture beaded the glass. Canadian bacon. Home fries. Bran flakes in cream with a sprinkle of blueberries on top—bloobies, her father had always called them, another one of those comic irrationalities that had irritated her mother out of all proportion.

———

CUJO

Dog Days French Toast Casserole

Makes 6 servings

A lot of terrible things happened in Castle Rock even before half the town got blown up, but the one that always makes me shiver is thinking of that poor young mother and her son trapped in their Pinto by that rabid St. Bernard, trying to find comfort in daydreams about family breakfasts.

This overnight French toast casserole is packed with cranberries and maple syrup and topped with a walnut streusel. Serve with a pitcher of orange juice and a fruit salad for a weekend or holiday breakfast that you can enjoy at the table with the family, instead of trapped at the stove.

1 large loaf bread (about 1½ pounds), preferably egg bread (see page 177) or brioche, cut into ½-inch slices

2½ cups fresh or frozen cranberries

2 cups milk

8 eggs

½ cup maple syrup, plus more for serving

Finely grated zest of 2 large oranges

1 teaspoon kosher salt

1 teaspoon vanilla extract

½ cup all-purpose flour

½ cup chopped walnuts

¼ cup rolled oats

3 tablespoons light brown sugar

1 teaspoon ground cinnamon

¼ cup cold butter, plus more for serving

Butter a 9 by 13-inch baking dish. Using half of the loaf, arrange half the bread slices in an even layer in the bottom of the prepared dish, cutting the slices to fit. Scatter half the cranberries evenly over the bread, then top with the remaining bread slices and remaining cranberries. Press down gently to settle the cranberries.

CONTINUED

In a large bowl, whisk together the milk, eggs, maple syrup, orange zest, salt, and vanilla. Pour evenly over the bread, cover tightly with plastic wrap, and refrigerate for at least 4 hours, or up to overnight.

Remove the dish from the refrigerator 30 minutes before baking. Position an oven rack on the middle rung and heat the oven to 350°F.

In a small bowl, stir together the flour, walnuts, oats, brown sugar, and cinnamon. Grate in the butter and, using your fingertips, gently work it into the flour mixture. Sprinkle this streusel across the top of the soaked bread.

Bake the casserole until golden, 45 to 55 minutes. Remove from the oven and cool on a wire rack for 10 minutes.

Cut the French toast into squares and serve, passing additional butter and maple syrup at the table.

"We're closed until lunch," he said, "but there's coffee."

"And a cinnamon roll?" Julia asked hopefully.

Barbie shook his head. "Rose didn't make them. Trying to conserve the gennie as much as possible."

"Makes sense," she said. "Just coffee, then."

He had carried the pot with him, and poured. "You look tired."

"Barbie, everyone looks tired this morning. And scared to death."

UNDER THE DOME

Apple-Cinnamon Rolls

Makes 12 rolls

Chester's Mill was cut off from the rest of Maine, and the world, just before noon on October 21. The military labeled it The Dome, and so it became Dome Day, and eventually, the Year of the Dome, though no one seems to remember the exact year it came down. Shame they couldn't have had fresh cinnamon rolls the next morning to soothe what must have been some frayed nerves, even for unshakable Yankees.

Start this recipe the night before for fresh, homemade apple-cinnamon rolls in the morning.

DOUGH

3¾ cups all-purpose flour

2½ teaspoons instant dry yeast

1 teaspoon kosher salt

¾ cup buttermilk (see "Buttermilk," page 6)

3 eggs

6 tablespoons butter, at room temperature

¼ cup granulated sugar

1 teaspoon vanilla extract

1 teaspoon vegetable oil

FILLING

2 medium apples (such as Cortland, Pink Lady, or Gala), peeled, cored, and chopped small

⅓ cup golden raisins

1 tablespoon ground cinnamon

1 teaspoon fresh lemon juice or white vinegar

2 tablespoons butter, melted

1 cup packed light brown sugar

ICING

2 cups powdered sugar

¼ cup buttermilk (see "Buttermilk," page 6)

1 teaspoon vanilla extract

CONTINUED

To make the dough: In a medium bowl, whisk together the flour, yeast, and salt.

In the bowl of a stand mixer fitted with the paddle attachment, combine the buttermilk, eggs, butter, granulated sugar, and vanilla. Mix on medium speed until well combined, then turn the speed to low and gradually add the flour, mixing to form a rough ball. Switch to the dough hook and knead the mixture on low speed for 6 to 8 minutes. The dough should be soft and tacky, but not sticky.

Pour the vegetable oil over the dough and roll it around in the bowl a few times to completely coat. Cover the bowl with a clean dish towel and then a plate. Set the bowl in a warm, draft-free place to rise for 1½ to 2 hours, until the dough is doubled in size and the dough springs back when poked.

To make the filling: In a small bowl, combine the apples, raisins, cinnamon, and lemon juice and toss together.

Butter a 9 by 13-inch ceramic or glass baking dish.

On a lightly floured work surface, using a rolling pin and even pressure, roll the dough out from the center in all four compass directions: north, south, east, and west. Turn and loosen the dough occasionally as you continue to roll it into an 18 by 12-inch rectangle. Leaving a ½-inch border on one long edge, brush the dough with the melted butter. Sprinkle with the brown sugar and then the apples.

Starting with the long end covered in filling, roll the dough into a tight, 18-inch-long log. Pinch the seam closed, then, using a serrated knife, saw the log into twelve 1½-inch portions. Arrange the rolls, spirals up, in the prepared baking dish. Cover with plastic wrap and refrigerate overnight, or up to 12 hours.

Take the rolls out of the fridge about 45 minutes before baking, loosening the plastic wrap so that they can rise freely, and set in a warm, draft-free place to rise until doubled in size.

Position an oven rack on the middle rung and heat the oven to 350°F.

Bake the rolls until they are puffed and light golden, 30 to 35 minutes. Transfer the dish to a wire rack to cool for 30 minutes.

To make the icing: In a medium bowl, stir together the powdered sugar, buttermilk, and vanilla until smooth and glossy.

Drizzle the icing across the rolls in the baking dish. Cut or pull apart into individual rolls and serve.

"I'd like a cheese and mushroom omelet," Ralph said.

"Uh-huh." She switched her cud from one side of her jaw to the other. "Two-egg or three-egg, hon?"

"Four, if that's okay."

She raised her eyebrows slightly and jotted on the pad. "Okay by me if it's okay by you. Anything with that?"

"Yes, please. A glass of o.j., large, an order of bacon, an order of sausage, and an order of home fries. Better make that a double order of home fries." He paused, thinking, then grinned. "Oh, and do you have any Danish left?"

INSOMNIA

Four-Egg Cheese and Mushroom Omelet

Makes 2 servings

There's nothing like a visit to the local diner for a breakfast that will set you up for the rest of the day, especially if you're trying to prevent another disaster in Derry. I will never understand why anyone settles in that deadly town.

There's also nothing like breakfast for supper when you're running low on gas in the early evening. Make a stack of toast to serve alongside while the omelet cooks.

1 tablespoon olive oil

3 tablespoons butter

6 button mushrooms, trimmed and thinly sliced

4 eggs

1 teaspoon kosher salt

¼ teaspoon freshly ground black pepper

½ cup shredded Cheddar cheese

1 green onion, white and green parts, thinly sliced

In a 7- or 8-inch cast-iron or nonstick skillet over medium-high heat, warm the olive oil with 1 tablespoon of the butter. When bubbling, add the mushrooms and cook until they have released their liquid and are just starting to brown, 7 to 10 minutes. Transfer to a plate and set aside. Wipe the skillet clean.

In a small bowl, whisk together the eggs, salt, and pepper. In the cleaned skillet over medium heat, melt the remaining 2 tablespoons butter and swirl the pan to coat the bottom. Add the eggs and, using a spatula, draw their edges toward the center of the pan, scrambling them lightly to form large curds. Shake and tilt the pan to return the eggs to an even layer across the bottom of the pan.

Cook until the edges of the egg just begin to set and the top of the omelet is still moist, about 1 minute. Sprinkle the cheese over one half of the eggs, and top with the mushrooms and green onion; run the spatula around the edge of the skillet to loosen the omelet. Cook until the cheese has started to melt and the bottom is lightly golden, 1 to 2 minutes more. Fold the plain half of the omelet over the filling.

Cut the omelet in half and divide onto two plates. Serve immediately.

A grease-spotted paper bag flew into the car and landed on the floor. He didn't see Mattie, only heard him: "Good luck, outlaw." Then the shadow was gone. . . .

Heaven was in that bag. He could smell it. Heaven turned out to be a cheese-and-sausage biscuit, a Hostess Fruit Pie, and a bottle of Carolina Sweetheart Spring Water. . . .

He thought if the train took a sudden yaw and it spilled, he would go insane. He gobbled the sausage biscuit in five snatching bites and chased it with another big swallow of water.

THE INSTITUTE

Sausage on Cheese Biscuits to Go

Makes 8 breakfast sandwiches

Sneaking out of an armed fortress in the woods works up an appetite, no doubt. In this recipe, homemade sausage patties are sweetened with maple syrup and sandwiched between light, but extraordinarily cheesy, biscuits.

CHEESE BISCUITS

2 cups all-purpose flour

2 teaspoons Bakewell Cream (see Note)

1 teaspoon baking soda

½ teaspoon kosher salt

½ cup cold butter

1 cup shredded aged Cheddar cheese

⅔ cup milk, plus 1 tablespoon

BREAKFAST SAUSAGE

1½ pounds ground pork

¼ cup quick-cooking oats or cornmeal

1½ tablespoons minced fresh sage

1½ tablespoons minced fresh parsley

1 tablespoon maple syrup

1½ teaspoons kosher salt

½ teaspoon freshly ground black pepper

¼ teaspoon red pepper flakes

¼ teaspoon freshly grated nutmeg

2 teaspoons vegetable oil

To make the biscuits: Position an oven rack on the lower-middle rung and heat the oven to 475°F. Line a baking sheet with parchment paper.

CONTINUED

In a large bowl, whisk together the flour, Bakewell Cream, baking soda, and salt. Grate the butter into the bowl and, using your fingertips, gently work it into the flour mixture, leaving a few lumps. Add ¾ cup of the cheese and toss to combine. Add the ⅔ cup milk and stir to form a soft ball of dough.

Transfer the dough to a lightly floured work surface and knead three or four times to bring it together. Pat the dough into a 6 by 12-inch rectangle about 1 inch thick. Using a knife, cut eight 3-inch square biscuits and arrange them on the prepared baking sheet about 1 inch apart. Brush the tops with the remaining 1 tablespoon milk, then sprinkle with the remaining ¼ cup cheese.

Bake the biscuits for 5 minutes, then turn off the oven. Leave the biscuits in the oven until they are golden brown, 5 to 10 minutes more. Transfer to a wire rack to cool slightly.

To make the breakfast sausage: In a large bowl, combine the pork, oats, sage, parsley, maple syrup, salt, black pepper, red pepper flakes, and nutmeg and mix well with your hands. Divide into eight equal portions, roll into balls, and flatten with your palm into 4-inch patties.

Line a plate with a double layer of paper towels.

In a large skillet over medium heat, warm the vegetable oil until shimmering. Add half the sausage patties and fry, flipping once, until cooked through and browned on both sides, 5 to 7 minutes. Transfer to the prepared plate to drain and repeat with the remaining sausage patties.

Split the biscuits and sandwich a sausage patty between the halves. Serve immediately.

Notes

No Bakewell Cream? Substitute 2 teaspoons baking powder and omit the baking soda.

To bake a batch of these biscuits in the morning without a lot of fuss, prepare and cut the unbaked dough into individual biscuits ahead of time. Place flat on a tray—don't let them touch—and freeze until firm. Bag them up and keep in the freezer for up to 1 month. To bake, heat the oven as directed, brush the frozen biscuits with milk, top with the cheese, and bake for 10 minutes before turning off the oven and leaving them in there until they are golden, 5 to 10 minutes more. You can also refrigerate the uncooked sausage patties for up to 1 day, or freeze for up to 1 month. Defrost in the refrigerator overnight before frying as directed.

After all, it wasn't like he was six anymore, when they had first come here to Maine to take care of Gramma, and he had cried with terror whenever Gramma held out her heavy arms toward him from her white vinyl chair that always smelled of the poached eggs she ate and the sweet bland powder George's mom rubbed into her flabby, wrinkled skin; she held out her white-elephant arms, wanting him to come to her and be hugged to that huge and heavy old white-elephant body. . . .

"GRAMMA"

Gramma's Crab Cake Brunch

Makes 4 servings

Almost every pantry in Maine has a package of saltine crackers on the shelves, and this traditional recipe goes to the heart of our best-kept-simple approach to food. The crab is the star, and the cracker crumbs and subtle seasonings let it shine.

I still pick young dandelions in the spring before their greens get bitter; they make a crunchy, peppery bed for the crab cake; and the silky yolk from a soft-poached, farm-fresh egg brings it all together for a simple, yet sophisticated brunch Gramma would devour.

5 eggs

Kosher salt

1½ cups saltine cracker crumbs (from about 1 sleeve of crackers; see Note)

¼ cup finely chopped green onions, white and light green parts

1 tablespoon mayonnaise

1 teaspoon fresh lemon juice

½ teaspoon Worcestershire sauce

¼ teaspoon cayenne pepper

8 ounces fresh or pasteurized lump-style crabmeat

Vegetable oil for frying

4 handfuls young dandelion greens or baby arugula

Freshly ground black pepper

3 tablespoons Nouveau French Dressing (page 230) or other vinaigrette

Set a fine-mesh sieve over a small bowl. One at a time, crack four of the eggs into the sieve. Discard the thinner, more liquid whites that fall through, then add the remaining, thicker whites and yolks to the same small bowl. (Treat them reasonably gently and they will remain intact and distinct, and now hold their shape better during poaching.) Set aside.

CONTINUED

In a large saucepan over medium heat, combine 3 inches of water with 1 teaspoon salt and bring to a slow simmer.

In a medium bowl, lightly beat the remaining egg. Add ¾ cup of the cracker crumbs, the green onions, mayonnaise, lemon juice, Worcestershire, and cayenne and stir together. Carefully fold in the crabmeat to avoid breaking up the lumps.

Pour the remaining ¾ cup cracker crumbs onto a large plate. Divide the crab mixture into four equal portions and form them into 3-inch cakes about 1 inch thick. Lightly dredge the cakes in the cracker crumbs until coated.

Line a plate with a double layer of paper towels.

In a large pan over medium heat, warm ¼ inch of vegetable oil until shimmering. Add the crab cakes and fry, turning once, until they are hot inside and a crisp golden brown on the outside, 6 to 7 minutes. Transfer to the prepared plate to drain.

One at a time, carefully pour the reserved eggs into the barely simmering water, gently pulling the bowl back each time one drops into the water—the closer you get the edge of the bowl to the simmering water, the easier this is. After 30 seconds, using a slotted spoon, gently turn the eggs a few times each. This will help shape them into ovals. Cook for 3 to 4 minutes for soft-poached eggs; the whites should be firm and the yolks plump and soft to the touch. If you prefer harder yolks, leave the eggs in for another minute or two until they're cooked to your preference. Using the slotted spoon, remove the eggs and gently blot on a paper towel or clean dish towel.

Put the greens in a large bowl, taste and lightly season with salt and pepper, and toss with the dressing.

Mound the greens on four plates and top each with a crab cake, then a poached egg. Serve immediately, passing salt and pepper at the table.

Notes

To make crumbs from the saltines, process the crackers in a food processor until they are evenly crushed into fine crumbs, about 30 seconds. If you prefer, substitute the same amount of fresh bread crumbs for the saltine crumbs.

The eggs can be poached up to 3 days ahead. Transfer to a bowl of ice water until cooled, then cover and chill, in the water, until needed. Reheat the eggs in gently simmering water for 1 minute before serving.

Dinner

It used to be the main meal of the day, but these days, dinner, or lunch as it's now more commonly called, is a quick meal meant to keep the hunger away until the day's work is done. A sandwich most likely, or, if you're lucky, a piece of leftover chicken wrapped in wax paper with a juicy apple from the cellar to wash it down.

Some of these recipes can be taken with you to work, like the salad; just make sure to pack the dressing separately to avoid everything getting soggy. As long as you have a thermos to keep them warm, any of the soups are good choices for lunch to go. When it's cold, the mild heat of the curry and cayenne in the mulligatawny really gets the blood pumping.

Others are a celebration of earlier times when the noon meal was the biggest of the day, like a Sunday boiled dinner. A traditional New England meal of a boiled corned beef and vegetables, similar to corned beef and cabbage, but also, in Maine at least, including potatoes, turnips, carrots, beets, and, sometimes, onion.

Boiled dinners are always best in early fall, at harvest-time, when the vegetables are fresh from the ground and everyone's hungry after working since dawn. That said, a boiled dinner served up in late winter with vegetables slightly shrunken from the cellar is always welcomed by everyone at the table, as is the red flannel hash for breakfast the next day. There's nothing like a boiled dinner for supper to keep you fed for days.

If you've got kids, it's hard to go wrong with American chop suey for a weekend dinner. My friend's mom, Mae, says we garbled *tsa tsui*, Mandarin for a little of this and that, into "chop suey" with our lazy English tongues. Beloved across New England and beyond, where variations are called everything from goulash to chili mac to macaroni red, it's more of a guideline than a recipe. Don't be afraid to use the leftover bits of this and that in your fridge to put it together, and always make lots—it tastes better the next day.

Whether you're around the table with family, or in the lunchroom where you do your nine-to-five, make sure you sit down for a spell and take time to breathe. There's nothing unhealthier than eating on the run or in the car, out of a bag. I never insisted on keeping with many of the old ways, but I always made sure that Ray and I sat down together for one meal a day. It kept my family together even as life, and the Major, took them from me.

Stephanie nodded. In this part of the world supper came early. Dinner—pronounced *dinnah*—was what you ate from your lunchpail at noon, often while out in your lobster boat.

THE COLORADO KID

"About that same time I started taking Health and Nutrition at school, and I found out you could eat just about all the raw green stuff you wanted and not gain weight. So one night my mother put on a salad with lettuce and raw spinach in it, chunks of apple and maybe a little leftover ham. Now I've never liked rabbit-food that much, but I had three helpings and just raved on and on to my mother about how good it was.

"That went a long way toward solving the problem. She didn't care so much *what* I ate as long as I ate a *lot* of it."

—
IT

Ben's Really Big Salad

Makes 1 serving (multiply for additional servings)

For Ben Hanscom, salad was a diet revolution, but parents and cooks everywhere have long been disguising leftovers as salads. One of the most famous, the Cobb salad, was supposedly created by a hungry, fridge-raiding Hollywood restaurateur during a late-night card game.

Get creative, keep your taste buds guessing, and shape up to battle the evil lying in wait beneath your own hometown.

2 cups washed mixed salad greens (such as lettuce, arugula, baby kale, spinach, escarole, and radicchio)

Kosher salt

Freshly ground black pepper

2 to 3 tablespoons Nouveau French Dressing (page 230), plus more for drizzling

1 cup fruits and vegetables (such as shredded carrot, cubed avocado, tomato slices, chunks of pear, cold steamed asparagus, and roasted bell peppers)

4 ounces protein (such as cooked or canned fish, shellfish, or chicken; hard-cooked eggs; and smoked tofu)

Garnishes (such as cheese, bacon, nuts or seeds, crispy fried onions, black olives, sliced green onions, and fresh herbs)

In a large bowl, toss the salad greens with a pinch each of salt and pepper. Add 2 tablespoons of the dressing and toss again, adding the remaining 1 tablespoon dressing if needed to coat all the greens lightly.

Mound the dressed greens on a plate. Top with your chosen fruits and vegetables and protein, taste and season with salt and pepper, and sprinkle with your garnishes. Drizzle with a little more dressing, if desired, before serving.

Jack Evans was in the kitchen, whipping eggs for a noontime frittata. LCD Soundsystem was playing—"North American Scum"—and Jack was singing along when a small voice spoke his name from behind him. He didn't at first recognize the voice as belonging to his wife of fourteen years; it sounded like the voice of a child. . . . Her left hand, clad in a filthy gardening glove, was cradling her right hand, and red stuff was running through the muddy fingers. . . . It was blood. Jack dropped the bowl he'd been holding. It shattered on the floor.

UNDER THE DOME

One-Handed Frittata

Makes 6 servings

Myra Evans was out in the garden behind her house, picking the last of the winter squash when the dome came down over Chester's Mill. Poor woman never knew what hit her—probably didn't even know part of the backyard was over the town line in Motton.

Easy enough to put together with one hand, this frittata combines the mild, comforting flavors of egg, leek, and potato with bites of strong, salty cheese. It makes a substantial dinner on its own; add a bowl of soup and you've got supper.

2 large leeks, white and light green parts

2 medium yellow potatoes (such as Carola or Yukon gold)

10 eggs

¼ cup milk

1½ teaspoons kosher salt

½ teaspoon freshly ground black pepper

3 tablespoons butter

1 garlic clove, finely grated or minced

½ cup crumbled goat or feta cheese

Position an oven rack on the upper-middle rung and heat the oven to 375°F.

Cut the leeks in half lengthwise, then cut them crosswise into ¼-inch slices. Rinse thoroughly in a bowl of cold water. Scoop out the leeks with your hands or a slotted spoon, leaving the grit and sand at the bottom of the bowl. Dry the leeks in a clean dish towel or salad spinner.

Peel the potatoes, then slice them in half lengthwise and cut crosswise into ¼-inch-thick slices.

CONTINUED

In a medium saucepan over high heat, combine the potatoes with 1 inch of cold water and bring to a boil. Turn the heat to low, cover the pot, and simmer the potatoes until fork-tender, 5 to 6 minutes. Drain and briefly toss in the pan so that the steam escapes and the potatoes dry. Set aside.

In a large bowl, whisk together the eggs, milk, salt, and pepper. Set aside.

In a 9-inch cast-iron pan or ovenproof skillet over medium heat, melt the butter. When it's bubbling, add the leeks and cook, stirring occasionally, until soft and translucent, 5 to 7 minutes. Add the garlic and potatoes and cook, stirring constantly, for 2 minutes more. Shake the pan to settle the vegetables in an even layer.

Pour the eggs over the potatoes and leeks and gently shake the pan to settle the eggs. Cook for 5 minutes without disturbing, then sprinkle the cheese over the top, transfer the skillet to the oven, and bake until the eggs are just set in the center, 15 to 18 minutes. Run a spatula around the edges and bottom of the pan, and slide the frittata onto a plate.

Cut the frittata into wedges and serve immediately.

The Derry of the Old Crocks was not the only secret city existing quietly within the place Ralph Roberts had always thought of as home; . . . Ralph had discovered there was . . . one that belonged strictly to the children. There were the abandoned hobo jungles near the railroad depot on Neibolt Street, where one could sometimes find tomato soup cans half-full of mulligatawny stew and bottles with a swallow or two of beer left in them; . . . there were the hundred . . . tangled trails winding through the Barrens, an overgrown valley which slashed through the center of town like a badly healed scar.

INSOMNIA

Better-than-Canned Mulligatawny

Makes 4 servings

Ralph Roberts knew his way around Derry better than just about anyone. From his childhood explorations in the Barrens and the railroad depot, site of the infamous Apocalyptic Rockfight, to the long walks he took along the Harris Avenue Extension during the summer his wife died, Ralph explored more of that ill-fated town on foot than anyone.

Long walks require fuel, and I don't mean from a can. The richest, tastiest, and most nutritious soups start with quality stock. Try Quick Chicken Stock for homemade chicken stock in record time.

3 tablespoons butter or refined coconut oil

1 medium yellow onion, julienned

1 medium carrot, diced

1 large celery stalk, diced

1½ tablespoons finely grated fresh ginger (see Note)

3 garlic cloves, finely grated (see Note)

1 tablespoon tomato paste

2 teaspoons curry powder (preferably Madras)

Cayenne pepper

4 cups chicken stock (see page 233) or vegetable stock

⅔ cup red lentils

1 cup coconut milk

1 tablespoon fresh lemon juice

Kosher salt

Chopped fresh cilantro leaves for garnishing

In a medium saucepan over medium heat, melt the butter. When it's bubbling, add the onion, carrot, and celery and cook, stirring occasionally, until softened and golden, 7 to 10 minutes.

CONTINUED

Add the ginger and garlic to the pan, stir, and cook until fragrant, about 30 seconds. Add the tomato paste, curry powder, and ¼ teaspoon cayenne. Cook, stirring constantly, until the butter is glistening, about 1 minute. Pour in the chicken stock and red lentils, stir, and bring to a boil. Turn the heat to low, cover, and simmer for 30 minutes.

Add the coconut milk and lemon juice to the pan and stir. Taste and season with salt and additional cayenne, then heat until steaming; do not allow the mulligatawny to boil.

Ladle the mulligatawny into bowls, garnish with cilantro, and serve immediately.

Note
Peel the ginger with the edge of a small spoon, then grate it on your kitchen rasp/Microplane. Tap the rasp on the side of the pan to release the ginger, then grate the garlic, which will clean the rasp of most of the clingy ginger bits. Tap the rasp on the side of the pan to release the garlic, then give it a quick rinse under hot water (dried garlic juice sticks like glue).

Potato and Collard Soup

Makes 6 servings

We never wanted for meat before Ray's daddy got himself carted off by the Squads. He had a big mouth, for sure, but he was a good shot, and we never went hungry. After he was gone, we had years of making do with less.

This vegan soup of creamy potatoes and silky collards is a delicious budget stretcher. Nutritional yeast gives it a kick of umami— or mouthfeel—that almost tricks your mind into thinking there's meat in there. Almost.

6 cups water

1½ pounds yellow potatoes (such as Carola or Yukon gold), peeled and cut into 2-inch pieces

1 large yellow onion, julienned

2 garlic cloves, quartered

¼ cup olive oil

2 bay leaves

1 bunch collard greens, washed and stemmed

1 tablespoon nutritional yeast (optional)

Kosher salt

Ground white pepper

In a large saucepan over high heat, combine the water, potatoes, onion, garlic, olive oil, and bay leaves. Bring to a boil, turn the heat to low, and simmer, uncovered, until the potatoes are very soft, about 30 minutes. Remove and discard the bay leaves, and, using an immersion blender, puree the soup until smooth.

Stack the collard leaves, three or four at a time, and roll into cigars. Slice crosswise into ¼-inch-wide strips, then roughly chop the strips. Add the collard greens, nutritional yeast (if using), 2 teaspoons salt, and ¼ teaspoon white pepper to the soup; simmer for another 20 minutes. Taste and season with additional salt and pepper, if desired.

Divide the soup among six bowls and serve hot.

Jacobs snapped his fingers in front of her eyes like a stage hypnotist. "Focus, Astrid. Who brought you here?"

"J—Jenny."

"What did you have for supper last night?"

"Sloop. Sloop and salad."

He snapped his fingers in front of her swimming eyes again. It made her blink and recoil. The muscles beneath her skin seemed to be tightening and firming even as I watched. It was wonderful and awful.

"Soup. Soup and salad."

REVIVAL

Sloop

Makes 6 servings

No one would ever praise the ex-reverend Jacobs for his bedside manner, nor his ethics, but the magic he worked with electricity was enough for those desperate for a miracle to seek him out. No doubt they all came to regret finding him.

Never mind an apple a day, have yourself a cup of this corn chowder to keep the ex-reverend Jacobs away. Flavored with bacon, full of vegetables, and made hearty with chicken stock and cream, it tastes even better the next day. Store leftovers in the fridge for up to 3 days; do not freeze. If you have any extra bacon fat, save it to start another batch of soup later in the week.

5 large ears fresh corn, shucked and cleaned of silk, or 4 cups fresh or frozen corn kernels

4 slices thick-cut bacon, cut crosswise into ¼-inch strips

1 large yellow onion, julienned

2 medium celery stalks, halved lengthwise and cut into ½-inch pieces

2 medium russet potatoes, peeled and cut into 1-inch wedges (see Note)

1 garlic clove, finely grated or minced

½ teaspoon Bell's Seasoning or other poultry seasoning

1 cup dry white wine

2 cups chicken stock (see page 233)

Kosher salt

Ground white pepper

½ cup whipping cream

Lay an ear of corn flat on a cutting board, with the stalk pointing toward you. Holding the ear firmly, slice the kernels off one side and turn the ear so it rests on the cut side. Slice the kernels off this side, repeating until all the cobs are clean of kernels.

CONTINUED

Line a plate with a double layer of paper towels.

Arrange the bacon pieces in one layer in a cold Dutch oven or large saucepan. Set over medium heat and render the fat from the bacon, stirring occasionally and lowering the heat as necessary to prevent burning. When the bacon is crisp, 7 to 10 minutes, scoop it from the pan with a slotted spoon, transfer to the prepared plate, and set aside. Pour off all but 2 tablespoons of fat from the pan.

Add the onion and celery to the bacon fat and fry, stirring occasionally, until soft and translucent, about 5 minutes. Add the corn kernels and cook, stirring, until they just start to turn golden, 8 to 10 minutes more. Add the potatoes, garlic, and Bell's and stir until aromatic, about 30 seconds. Add the wine and deglaze the pan by scraping up the browned bits with a wooden spoon, then reduce the liquid, stirring occasionally, until the pan is almost dry, 3 to 5 minutes. Add the chicken stock, 1 teaspoon salt, and ½ teaspoon white pepper; lower the heat; and simmer until the potatoes are very soft, about 20 minutes.

Transfer four ladles of cooked vegetables to a blender. Add two ladles of mostly broth and blend on high speed until pureed, 1 to 2 minutes. Pour back into the soup pot, stir in the cream, turn the heat to medium, and reheat gently until steaming. Taste and season with additional salt and pepper.

Ladle the corn chowder into bowls, garnish with the crisp bacon, and serve piping hot.

Note
Cut the potatoes into small wedges, so that one side is thicker than the other. The thin side will cook off into the chowder, thickening it without the use of flour.

George flicked on the kitchen light, even though it really wasn't
dark enough for it yet. Then he turned on LO HEAT under his macaroni.
His thoughts kept returning to Gramma, sitting in her white vinyl
chair like a big fat worm in a dress, her corona of hair every crazy
whichway on the shoulders of her pink rayon robe, holding out her
arms for him to come, him shrinking back against his Mom, bawling.

"GRAMMA"

Killer Mac and Cheese

Makes 6 servings

Uncooked pasta is stirred into a cheesy cream sauce enriched with chicken stock, resulting in a one-pot, flavor-filled comfort meal that will drive away even the most frightening night—or day—mares about the scariest of grammas.

Store leftovers in the fridge for up to 3 days. To incorporate more vegetables, add 2 medium stalks of minced celery and 1 cup of tiny cauliflower florets to the pan with the onion.

¾ cup panko-style bread crumbs

½ cup grated Parmesan cheese

1 tablespoon olive oil

¼ cup butter

1 medium yellow onion, julienned

¼ cup all-purpose flour

2 cups chicken stock (see page 233)

2 cups milk

3 cups shredded aged Cheddar cheese

1 cup whipping cream

1½ teaspoons kosher salt

1 teaspoon mustard powder

¼ teaspoon ground white pepper

1 pinch cayenne pepper

3 cups dried macaroni

Position an oven rack on the middle rung and heat the oven to 350°F. In a small bowl, toss together the bread crumbs, Parmesan, and olive oil; set aside.

In a Dutch oven over medium heat, melt the butter. Add the onion and fry, stirring occasionally, until soft and translucent, 5 to 7 minutes. Stir in the flour and cook, stirring constantly, for 1 minute.

CONTINUED

Whisk the chicken stock and milk into the flour, turn the heat to medium-high, and bring to a low boil, stirring occasionally, until the sauce is thick enough to coat the back of a spoon, 7 to 10 minutes.

Add the Cheddar, a couple handfuls at a time, to the pot and stir until it has all been incorporated and the sauce is smooth. Stir in the cream, salt, mustard powder, white pepper, and cayenne. Add the macaroni and cook, stirring frequently, until the pasta begins to swell and no longer sticks to the bottom of the pot, 2 to 3 minutes.

Transfer the uncovered Dutch oven to the oven and bake the macaroni for 30 minutes, then top with the Parmesan bread crumbs and return to the oven until golden and bubbling, about 15 minutes more. Remove from the oven and allow to rest for 10 minutes on a wire rack.

Spoon the macaroni and cheese onto plates and serve immediately.

They never used the Frisbee they had brought as camouflage; they
were too preoccupied. Nor did it matter. Few of the townspeople
heading back to their homes bothered looking into the Common.
A few were hurt. Most were carrying liberated foodstuffs, and some
were wheeling loaded shopping carts. Almost all looked ashamed
of themselves.

By noon, Joe and his friends were ready to give up. They were
also hungry.

"Let's go to my house," Joe said. "My mom'll make us something
to eat."

"Great," Benny said. "Hope it's chop suey. Your ma's chop suey
is tight."

UNDER THE DOME

American Chop Suey

Makes 6 servings

Once upon a time, it was rare to find a Maine family, or a school cafeteria for that matter, who didn't have their own recipe for this New England staple. Chop suey always tastes best when it's made from random bits and pieces in the refrigerator and pantry—it's one of those recipes you can always find the ingredients for, even when you're locked down under a dome.

Some serve it topped with Parmesan, but I've always preferred a few crispy onions.

1½ cups dried macaroni

1 tablespoon vegetable oil

1 pound 90% lean ground beef

1 teaspoon kosher salt

½ teaspoon freshly ground black pepper

½ teaspoon garlic powder (optional)

1 cup diced yellow onion

½ cup diced green bell pepper

½ cup diced celery

One 28-ounce can stewed or whole tomatoes

3 tablespoons tomato paste

1 cup water, or as needed

Grated Parmesan cheese and/or crispy fried onions for serving

Bring a large pot of generously salted water to a boil. Add the macaroni and cook until al dente, 8 to 10 minutes. Drain, return to the pot, and cover to keep warm.

In a Dutch oven or other large, heavy pot over high heat, warm the vegetable oil until shimmering. Add the ground beef, breaking it up with your hands as you put it in the pot. Season with the salt, black pepper, and garlic powder (if using). Cook, continuing to break up the beef with the back of a wooden spoon, until browned, 6 to 8 minutes. Drain all but 2 tablespoons of the fat from the pot.

Turn the heat to medium and add the onion, bell pepper, and celery to the pot. Cook, stirring occasionally, until the vegetables are softened, about 5 minutes. Stir in the canned tomatoes, tomato paste, water, and macaroni. Bring to a boil, then lower the heat and simmer for 15 minutes, adding more water if necessary to prevent it from drying out.

Divide the chop suey onto plates or into bowls, and serve, passing the Parmesan and/or crispy onions at the table.

He looked from me to the hatchet and then back to me again. The look
of surprise on his face would have been comical if the business hadn't
been so serious.

"Then, once it's done, you better heat up that boiled dinner and help
yourself to some more of it," I told him. "Eat til you bust, because
you'll be goin to jail and I ain't heard they serve anything good and
home-cooked in jail. You'll be over in Belfast to start with, I guess.
I bet they got one of those orange suits just your size."

DOLORES CLAIBORNE

Sunday Boiled Dinner

Makes 8 servings

She may have been a fool when she married
Joe Claiborne straight out of high school,
but Dolores eventually smartened up when
she had more than just herself to protect.
Recollections of the hatchet incident held
him at bay until she had finally had enough
to end him once and for all.

Despite its resemblance to dead flesh,
Mainers prefer the softer, sweeter meat
of gray-colored, "fresh" corned beef over
the nitrate-cured pink version seen most
everywhere else, but I reckon either tastes
just as good.

4 pounds corned beef

12 black peppercorns

2 whole cloves

2 bay leaves

1 teaspoon mustard seeds (optional)

4 small turnips, peeled and quartered

16 small new potatoes, cut in half if larger

4 large carrots, peeled and cut into
3-inch lengths

1 large yellow onion, cut into 8 wedges

1 medium cabbage head, outside leaves
discarded, cored, cut into 8 wedges

12 small beets, trimmed

½ teaspoon kosher salt

3 tablespoons butter

Rinse the corned beef to remove the brine. In a Dutch oven or other large, heavy pot, cover the corned beef with cold water. Bring to a boil over high heat, then lower the heat and simmer for 10 minutes. Using a small strainer, skim the gray scum off the surface of the water. Add the peppercorns, cloves, bay leaves, and mustard seeds (if using). Cover and simmer until the meat is tender, about 3 hours.

Add the turnips, potatoes, carrots, and onion to the Dutch oven and simmer, covered, for 20 minutes, then add the cabbage. Cover and simmer for 15 minutes more. Use the strainer to scoop out and discard the bay leaves, peppercorns, and cloves.

Meanwhile, in a large saucepan over medium-high heat, combine the beets, salt, and 2 inches of cold water. Cover and bring to a boil, then lower to a simmer and cook until tender, about 30 minutes. Drain and then, when cool enough to handle, peel the beets. Return to the pot and cover to keep warm.

Slice the corned beef thinly against the grain. Arrange down the center of a large serving platter. Surround the beef with the vegetables, including the beets. Dot the vegetables with the butter, and ladle some cooking liquid over top to warm up everything.

Serve the boiled dinner, passing more cooking liquid at the table.

Note
Red Flannel Hash is many Mainers' favorite by-product of a big boiled dinner. Chop the leftover vegetables and combine them, including the beets, in a large baking dish. Dot with butter and add some of the leftover cooking liquid. Cover and store in the fridge for up to 3 days. When ready to cook, uncover and bake at 350°F for about 1 hour. Serve with the leftover corned beef and paired with cheese biscuits (see page 27).

Supper

Mainers were farmers, foresters, and fishermen for centuries, and, by tradition, dinner was our big meal of the day. Stews and chowders bubbled away on the woodstove all morning while our men and women worked the land and sea; they ate heartily at midday to fuel their labor through sundown. Supper, on the other hand, was lighter, eaten in the evening once the last of the chores were done and the family was settled inside for the night.

Over the years, that changed as we surrendered our way of life, and our livelihoods. We were lured away from the land to work in factories and bland, fluorescent-lit offices where we ate quick and fast from the lunch pails we brought with us. That's when supper became the main meal, and the only time of day the family has a chance to all eat together. Supper comes early in Maine. Those from away may say different, but here, as my mama said, dinner's at noon, and you're late for supper if you're at the table after six o'clock.

Almost from the time I was able, I stood beside my mother on my stool at the kitchen counter, where she taught me everything she knew about cooking. Mama's roast beef is my favorite. She always seasoned it and put it in the fridge just before bed on Friday night for supper on Sunday. The poultry seasoning, Bell's if you can get it, seeps deep into the meat, and lends the gravy great flavor. Try to save some leftovers for sandwiches the next day.

Mind you, tastes also move on with time, and Mama wasn't the only one I learned from in the kitchen. New people brought different foods to Maine, and our taste buds are the better for it. Barbecue from the South, pizza and Bolognese from Italy, beef stewed in red wine from France, and delicately braised wings from China. Mae, my best friend's mom whose family owned a Chinese American diner near Portland, taught me the recipe for those. I was always in her kitchen, helping cook for parties. She taught me how to cut up the wings, and to save the drummettes for the fryer, and the tips for chicken stock.

I picked up the recipe for seekh kebabs from a traveler who came to watch the boys Walk. My mouth waters just thinking of that spiced, fatty meat crisping up on the grill—ten times tastier than those Pioneer Drumsticks of unseasoned, half-raw ground beef those boys gobbled down in Castle Rock all those years ago.

Hungry? Enough talking—it's time for *suppah*. Sit yourself down and eat well.

This is six o'clock, the supper hour (in the Lot, dinner is eaten at noon and the lunch buckets that men grab from counters before going out the door are known as dinner pails). . . . In Eva's the men are getting together whatever they have to get together: TV dinners, canned corned beef, canned beans which are woefully unlike the beans their mothers used to bake all Saturday morning and afternoon years ago. . . .

'SALEM'S LOT

So they ate . . . and they ate long and well. Like that old joke about the condemned man, Bill thought, but his own appetite was better than it had been in ages . . . since he was a kid, he was tempted to think. . . . The six of them began trading stuff back and forth—spareribs, moo goo gai pan, chicken wings that had been delicately braised, egg rolls, water chestnuts wrapped in bacon, strips of beef that had been threaded onto wooden skewers.

IT

Delicately Braised Wings

Makes 4 appetizer servings

For a change from fried, this recipe uses the red cooking method from Shanghai, braising the chicken wings in a dark, sticky sauce. Auntie Mae always had the Shaoxing wine, dark soy sauce, and rock sugar on hand, but these wings are delicious even if you have to substitute.

Don't skip the blanching stage; it renders some of the fat as well as impurities, such as blood, from the wings, resulting in an unblemished sauce. It's not traditional, but I like to finish them under the broiler to crisp up the skin.

16 chicken mid-joint wings (flat tops)

1 tablespoon vegetable oil

2 garlic cloves, halved

1-inch piece ginger, peeled and quartered

2 whole star anise

1-inch piece cinnamon stick

½ cup water

¼ cup Shaoxing wine (see Note)
or dry sherry

1½ tablespoons soy sauce

1½ tablespoons dark soy sauce (see Note)

1 tablespoon Chinese rock sugar (see Note), crushed, or 2 teaspoons granulated sugar

Green onions, white and green parts, finely chopped, for garnishing

Fill a medium saucepan halfway with water and bring to a boil over high heat. Add the chicken wings and blanch until the blood and other impurities float to the surface, 3 to 5 minutes. Drain and rinse the wings.

Position an oven rack 6 inches below the top element of the oven and heat the broiler.

CONTINUED

In a large ovenproof skillet over medium-high heat, warm the vegetable oil until shimmering. Add the wings and fry, turning occasionally, until both sides are golden, 7 to 10 minutes. Scatter the garlic, ginger, star anise, and cinnamon stick among the wings and stir until fragrant, about 1 minute. Pour in the ½ cup water, wine, and both soy sauces. Bring to a boil, then lower the heat and simmer briskly until the sauce is syrupy and reduced by about half, turning the wings occasionally, 12 to 15 minutes.

Add the sugar to the pan and toss gently. Flip all the wings top-side up; discard the garlic, ginger, star anise, and cinnamon; and transfer to the oven. Broil until the skin is bubbling and the sauce is reduced to a glossy coat on the wings, about 2 minutes.

Transfer the wings to a plate, garnish with the green onions, and serve immediately.

Notes

Shaoxing wine is also known as Chinese cooking wine. It's found in large grocery stores and Asian markets.

Dark soy sauce is found in Asian markets and online. Substitute with 1½ tablespoons soy sauce mixed with 1 teaspoon molasses and ¼ teaspoon granulated sugar.

Chinese rock sugar, which is also found in Asian markets and online, is less sweet than granulated sugar and gives sauces an appetizing, glossy translucence.

Blue Plate Special

Makes 4 servings

Travel back to the days when flatlanders came to Maine for vacation rather than grim spectacle; when diners were the kings of the road and the fastest food you could get was the Blue Plate Special, like this play on an open-faced hot turkey sandwich.

If you're short on time, prepare a package of store-bought stuffing to get supper on the table faster.

4 boneless, skin-on chicken thighs (see Note)

Kosher salt

3 tablespoons all-purpose flour

2½ cups chicken stock (see page 233) or water

2 thyme sprigs

Freshly ground black pepper

2 tablespoons butter

1 small yellow onion, julienned

2½ cups green peas, thawed if frozen

4 cups Potato Stuffing (page 166; see Note)

Position an oven rack on the middle rung and heat the oven to 300°F.

Season the chicken thighs liberally with salt.

In a large, cold cast-iron skillet, arrange the chicken thighs skin-side down. Set over medium heat and cook, untouched, until the skin is browned and crisp and releases from the pan with just a bit of coaxing from a spatula, about 15 minutes. Turn the chicken and cook until the juices run clear and an instant-read thermometer inserted into the thickest part of the meat (but not touching the bone) registers 165°F—anywhere from 2 to 10 minutes, depending on the thickness of the thighs.

CONTINUED

Using tongs, move the chicken to an ovenproof plate, skin-side up, leaving the fat in the pan. Transfer the chicken to the oven to keep warm.

Return the pan to medium heat and whisk the flour into the fat. Cook, stirring constantly, for 1 minute. Whisk in 2 cups of the chicken stock, add the thyme, turn the heat to high, and bring to a boil, stirring frequently. Turn the heat to a simmer and cook until this gravy thickens, 4 to 5 minutes, then remove from the heat. Taste and season with salt and pepper. Cover to keep warm.

In a medium saucepan over medium-high heat, melt the butter until bubbling. Add the onion and cook until soft and translucent, about 3 minutes. Add the peas, remaining ½ cup chicken stock, and ½ teaspoon salt; bring to a boil; and cook until the peas are tender, 3 to 5 minutes, then drain.

Remove and discard the thyme from the gravy and transfer to a bowl or gravy boat.

Spoon the stuffing onto plates, top with the chicken thighs, and add the peas and onions alongside. Serve immediately, passing the gravy at the table.

Notes

Chicken thighs are easy to debone. Watch an instructional video online, then save the bones to make chicken stock.

Whether you make the stuffing just before preparing the chicken thighs or pull it from the fridge, cover with aluminum foil and place in the 350°F oven until ready to serve.

When Ellie came down that night in her pajamas to be kissed, she asked Louis if Mrs. Crandall would go to heaven. She almost whispered the question to Louis, as if she understood it would be better if they were not overheard. Rachel was in the kitchen making a chicken pie, which she intended to take over to Jud the next day.

PET SEMATARY

Rotisserie Chicken Pie

Makes one 9-inch deep-dish pie

Time was, we only ate a chicken after it was done with laying, but now you can turn the modern conveniences of a store-bought rotisserie chicken and piecrusts into a delicious Down East classic from generations past.

If you end up with a little leftover filling, enjoy it on buttered toast for a quick cook's lunch.

2 tablespoons butter

2 tablespoons vegetable oil

1 small yellow onion, julienned

1 medium celery stalk, diced

1 small carrot, peeled and diced

1 garlic clove, finely grated or minced

2 teaspoons fresh thyme leaves, chopped, or 1 teaspoon dried thyme

¼ cup all-purpose flour

2 cups chicken stock (see page 233)

2 cups shredded meat from a rotisserie chicken, dark and white meat mixed

1 small russet potato, peeled and diced

½ cup green peas

Kosher salt

Freshly ground black pepper

Two 9-inch deep-dish piecrusts (see Note), at room temperature

1 egg beaten with 1 teaspoon water

In a large saucepan over medium-high heat, warm the butter and vegetable oil until bubbling. Add the onion, celery, and carrot and cook until the vegetables are soft, stirring occasionally and lowering the heat as needed to prevent them from browning, 5 to 7 minutes. Add the garlic and thyme and stir until fragrant, about 30 seconds.

Sprinkle the flour into the saucepan and stir constantly for 1 minute. Keep stirring and pour in the chicken stock, turning the heat to medium-high when the mixture begins to gently boil and thicken enough to coat the back of a spoon, 2 to 3 minutes more. Stir in the shredded chicken, potato, and peas; turn the heat to medium-low; and simmer gently for 15 minutes. Remove from the heat, then taste and season with salt and pepper.

Position an oven rack on the bottom rung and heat the oven to 375°F. If not packaged in pie tins, transfer one of the piecrusts into a 9-inch deep-dish pie tin and, using your fingertips, press it into the corners and sides of the tin. Remove the remaining piecrust from its packaging, and using a rolling pin, gently roll it flat if necessary.

Pour the filling into the piecrust in the tin and brush the top edge with some of the beaten egg. Lay the other piecrust across the top, crimp the top and bottom crusts together with your fingers or a fork, and use a knife to trim off any excess dough. Brush the crust with beaten egg, and poke the tip of a sharp knife into the top two or three times to create steam vents.

Bake the pie until the top crust is golden and the filling is bubbling through the vents, about 45 minutes. Let cool on a wire rack for 10 minutes.

Slice the chicken pie and serve.

Note
If you prefer homemade piecrust, prepare a double recipe of Short Crust Pastry (page 231).

Ralph thought of eating three scientifically balanced meals a day for
the rest of his life—no more sausage pizzas from Gambino's, no more
Coffee Pot sandwiches, no more chiliburgers from Mexico Milt's—and
found the prospect almost unbearably grim.

INSOMNIA

Sausage Pizza from Gambino's

Makes one 12-inch pizza

I can't get enough of old community
and church cookbooks; there's always
one keeper of a recipe in each one.
The American Legion Post 47 Ladies'
Auxiliary Cookbook from Derry—damn
that town—is a real gem.

They must have charmed Mr. Gambino
something fine for him to give up his
recipes for his thin crust and Italian red
sauce. Derry folk have a way of taking
what's yours.

2½ cups 00 durum flour or all-purpose flour
(see Note)

¾ teaspoon instant yeast

½ teaspoon kosher salt

¾ cup plus 1 tablespoon lukewarm
(95°F) water

1 tablespoon olive oil, plus 1 teaspoon

2 Italian sausages (about 3 ounces each)

½ cup Italian Red Sauce (page 229)
or other pizza sauce

About 1 cup shredded or torn
mozzarella cheese

Your favorite pizza toppings (such as
olives, mushrooms, bell peppers, onions,
or Parmesan cheese)

In a large bowl, stir together the flour, yeast, and
salt. Add the water and 1 tablespoon olive oil,
mixing with your hands until a rough ball forms.
Transfer the dough to a work surface and knead,
flouring the surface lightly, if necessary, to prevent sticking, until you have a soft, smooth dough
that is tacky but not sticky, about 5 minutes.

Clean and dry the bowl and add the remaining
1 teaspoon olive oil to it.

Return the dough to the bowl, rolling it in the
oil to coat. Cover the bowl with a clean dish towel
and then a plate. Set the bowl in a warm, draft-
free place to rise until the dough is one-and-a-half
times its original size, about 45 minutes.

CONTINUED

Position an oven rack on the bottom rung, place a pizza stone or baking sheet on the rack, and heat the oven to 550°F. Line a plate with a double layer of paper towels.

Meanwhile, transfer the dough to a work surface and knead eight to ten times to completely remove the air. Return the dough to the bowl, cover, and rest for 30 minutes to allow the gluten to relax; this will make rolling easier.

Remove the sausages from the casing and roll the meat into small balls. Set a medium skillet over medium-high heat, add the sausage, and brown on all sides, about 5 minutes. Transfer to the prepared plate to drain.

Transfer the dough to a large piece of parchment paper. Using a rolling pin and turning the dough occasionally, roll out the dough to a circle about 12 inches in diameter, or a shape that fits the pizza stone heating in the oven. Spread the red sauce over the dough and arrange the mozzarella, sausage, and other toppings on top. Using a pizza peel or another baking sheet, transfer the pizza to the pizza stone.

Bake the pizza until the cheese is golden and bubbling and the crust is browned, even charred in spots, 12 to 14 minutes. Let the pizza rest on a cutting board for 5 minutes.

Slice the pizza and serve.

Note

The higher the protein content of the flour, the more gluten is produced when it is mixed with water to create dough. North American 00 durum flour averages about 12 percent protein, putting it between all-purpose flour (about 11 percent) and bread flour (about 13 percent). The fine grind results in a silky dough that transforms into a chewy pizza crust with slightly puffed and charred edges, provided your oven is sufficiently hot.

For a moment I felt as if I had flipped back in time to the years
when I could tell my age with a single number. My family was crowded
around the dining room table just as they had been in the sixties,
all talking at once, laughing and squabbling, passing pork chops,
mashed potatoes, and a platter covered with a damp dishtowel: corn
on the cob, kept warm just as my mother used to do it.

REVIVAL

Mother Morton's Pork Chops

Makes 4 servings

Lean cuts of pork, like chops, can dry out quickly in the pan. Rendering the fat from the cap at the start produces juices for basting that keep the meat tender and juicy, resulting in comfort food to revive your very soul.

My boys always loved this dish served with Fettuccini Alfredo (page 132) for a delicious and substantial, midweek supper.

Note
Resting meat allows its juices to return to the center of the cut. During the rest, the internal temperature of the meat will rise at least 5 degrees to 145°F, a food-safe temperature for pork.

Three 1½-inch-thick boneless rib-end pork chops with fat caps (8 to 9 ounces each)
Kosher salt
Freshly ground black pepper
2 rosemary sprigs
2 garlic cloves, smashed
3 tablespoons butter

Season the pork chops, including the fat, liberally with salt and pepper. Set the chops in a large, cold skillet, standing on their fat caps. Set over medium-high heat and fry until each cap is crisp and golden and the fat is shimmering in the pan, 4 to 5 minutes.

Turn the heat to medium, lay the pork chops flat, and cook until the bottoms are golden brown, about 1 minute. Turn the chops and cook on the other side for 1 minute before turning again. Repeat, turning every 1 minute, basting occasionally, until the pork is dark golden brown and an instant-read thermometer registers 140°F, 8 to 10 minutes.

Remove the skillet from the heat and transfer the pork chops to a cutting board. Lightly tent with aluminum foil and allow to rest for 5 minutes. Add the rosemary, garlic, and butter to the skillet, off heat, and swirl to melt.

Slice the chops into ½-inch-thick pieces and serve, spooning the butter and drippings over top.

THE TOMMYKNOCKERS

Whopper Spareribs

Makes 6 servings

Daddy used to pick up racks of these Memphis dry-rubbed ribs in Augusta on his way back to Pownal from Down East. I've never left Maine, never mind been to Tennessee, but I can't imagine any ribs more tender or better tasting.

They cooked them low and slow, and added some Bell's in the rub for a New England twist. So good, there's no need for sauce on the side.

3 racks Kansas City–style pork side ribs (about 2 pounds per rack)

1½ tablespoons kosher salt

6 tablespoons Memphis Dry Rub (recipe follows), plus more for sprinkling (optional)

¼ cup apple cider vinegar

¼ cup water

Using paper towels, pat both sides of the racks dry. Using a butter knife or spoon, coax up the edge of the thin membrane from the back of each rack; then, using a paper towel, grasp and pull it all off to improve the flavor and tenderness of the finished ribs. Season both sides of each rack evenly with the salt and let stand at room temperature for 30 minutes.

Prepare the smoker and heat to 275°F. As the smoker comes to temperature, season both sides of each rack with the dry rub.

Put the ribs, meat-side up, in the smoker and smoke until the meat is tender to the touch and pulls away from the bones on the ends, 3 to 3½ hours. At 2 hours, in a small bowl, stir together the vinegar and water and then brush the racks with the mixture every 30 minutes.

CONTINUED

Transfer the racks to a baking sheet. Brush the vinegar-water on both sides of the ribs, and, if desired, sprinkle with more dry rub as well.

Slice the ribs between the bones and serve.

Variation

To cook the ribs in the oven, position an oven rack on the middle rung and heat the oven to 275°F. Line a rimmed baking sheet with parchment paper and arrange the ribs, meat-side up, on the baking sheet and cook and serve as directed.

Memphis Dry Rub

Makes about ¾ cup

Use on spareribs and BBQ pork chops or chicken.

¼ cup granulated sugar
¼ cup packed dark brown sugar
3 tablespoons sweet paprika
1 tablespoon garlic powder
2 teaspoons freshly ground black pepper
2 teaspoons ground ginger
1½ teaspoons onion powder
1 teaspoon Bell's Seasoning
or ground oregano

In a medium bowl, combine both sugars, the paprika, garlic powder, pepper, ground ginger, onion powder, and Bell's and stir to incorporate.

Store in a tightly sealed container at room temperature for up to 3 months.

When the flames began to die back a little bit, I stuck the sticks holding the Pioneer Drumsticks firmly into the ground at an angle over the fire. We sat around watching them as they shimmered and dripped and finally began to brown. Our stomachs made pre-dinner conversation.

Unable to wait until they were really cooked, we each took one of them, stuck it in a roll, and yanked the hot stick out of the center. They were charred outside, raw inside, and totally delicious. We wolfed them down and wiped the grease from our mouths with our bare arms.

"THE BODY"

Pioneer Drumsticks

Makes 6 servings

A lot has changed in Maine since those boys from Castle Rock walked along the train tracks to the watershed moment of their childhood. Immigrants to Maine from around the world have followed their dreams here, bringing with them a taste of home. There are also travelers who come to watch the boys on the Walk, and I listen and gather their stories and recipes too. The recipe for these seekh kebabs came from one of those travelers, long ago, when I still had all *my* boys around me. They were never happier than after a supper of these.

Serve with flatbreads and a green salad for a picnic-style meal that will take you back to the campfires under the stars of your youth.

1 small yellow onion, quartered

3 garlic cloves, quartered

1½-inch piece ginger, peeled and thinly sliced

2 teaspoons ground cumin

2 teaspoons ground coriander

2 teaspoons kosher salt

½ teaspoon freshly ground black pepper

½ teaspoon cayenne pepper

1½ pounds 80% lean ground beef

1 tablespoon fresh lime juice, plus lime wedges for serving

In the bowl of a small food processor, combine the onion, garlic, ginger, cumin, coriander, salt, black pepper, and cayenne and process until finely ground, 20 to 30 seconds, scraping down the bowl as needed.

In a large bowl, combine the beef with the spice mixture. Using your hands, blend together, massaging the spice mixture into the meat and pounding it into a paste with your fist. Cover and refrigerate for 30 minutes.

CONTINUED

Prepare the grill. If using charcoal, spread a chimney of hot coals evenly over the grill bed. For gas, set all burners to high and heat, covered, for 10 to 15 minutes.

Divide the meat into six equal portions about 4 ounces each. Roll each portion into a tight ball, then into a log about 8 inches long. Thread a metal or wooden skewer lengthwise through the center of each and, using your fingertips, press and roll the logs firmly onto the skewers.

Using a grill brush or stone, scrub the grill clean, if necessary. Squeeze three or four paper towels into a loose ball, drizzle with vegetable oil, and quickly wipe the grill to grease it.

Grill the skewers, covered, using tongs to turn them twice, until well charred and firm to the touch, 5 to 7 minutes. Transfer to a plate and let rest for 5 minutes.

Brush the lime juice onto the skewers and serve with the lime wedges for squeezing.

Note

I prefer the indestructibility of metal skewers; if you're using the wooden variety, be sure to soak them in water for 2 to 3 hours before grilling.

The front door opened directly on a small living room furnished
in Early American Junk Shop and dominated by an incredibly ancient
Motorola TV. A KLH sound system with quad speakers was putting out
the music.

Matt came out of the kitchen, outfitted in a red-and-white checked
apron. The odor of spaghetti sauce wandered out after him.

"Sorry about the noise," Matt said. "I'm a little deaf. I turn it up."

'SALEM'S LOT

Matt Burke's Bolognese

Makes 6 servings

This is a traditional Bolognese with the luxurious addition of pancetta and enough garlic to fill the mouth of the nearest undead. Simmered in milk to tenderize, then white wine for flavor before the tomatoes are added for a final three-hour simmer.

Serve with homemade pasta (see page 232), in a meaty lasagna, or in a bowl by itself with a heaping pile of Parmesan for company.

3 tablespoons butter

2 ounces pancetta, diced

2 tablespoons minced yellow onion

2 tablespoons minced red bell pepper

2 tablespoons minced celery

1 tablespoon finely grated or minced garlic

12 ounces 80% lean ground beef

Kosher salt

1 cup milk

1 cup dry white wine

One 28-ounce can whole tomatoes, with juices (see Note)

In a Dutch oven or other large, heavy pot over medium heat, melt the butter until bubbling. Add the pancetta, onion, bell pepper, celery, and garlic and cook, stirring occasionally, until the onion and celery are softened and translucent, about 5 minutes. Add the ground beef and ½ teaspoon salt, using the back of a wooden spoon to break up the beef. Cook, continuing to break up the meat, until it no longer looks raw but has not started to brown, 3 to 5 minutes.

CONTINUED

Add the milk to the beef and simmer until the liquid has evaporated, 15 to 20 minutes. Add the wine and simmer until it has evaporated, 15 to 20 minutes more. Add the tomatoes with their juices and bring to a simmer, breaking up the tomatoes with the wooden spoon. Turn the heat to low and simmer very gently, with just an occasional bubble at the surface, until most of the liquid has evaporated, 2½ to 3 hours. Taste and season with salt.

Serve the Bolognese warm.

Note

This recipe really shines when you use quality ingredients. Buy the best canned tomatoes you can find; those grown in Italy or California make the best sauce.

Keeton went on chowing into his boof borgnine, or whatever it was the Froggies called it, with great appetite. The reason for his happiness was simple. Every horse he had picked yesterday afternoon with the help of Winning Ticket had come in for him last night. Even Malabar, the thirty-to-one shot in the tenth race. He had come back to Castle Rock not so much driving as floating on air, with better than eighteen thousand dollars stuffed into his overcoat pockets.

NEEDFUL THINGS

Short Rib Borgnine

Makes 4 servings

This updated version of the French classic Beef Bourguignon uses bone-in short ribs and a full-bodied red wine for a rich, flavorful sauce. The crispy pancetta and buttery garlic crouton garnishes make for a decadent special-occasion meal that is the perfect way to celebrate your own Winning Ticket.

4 pounds bone-in beef short ribs, trimmed

Kosher salt

Freshly ground black pepper

2 tablespoons olive oil

1 large yellow onion, roughly chopped

2 large celery stalks, roughly chopped

2 medium carrots, peeled and roughly chopped, plus 12 baby carrots, halved lengthwise, or quartered if large

1 garlic head, cloves smashed and peeled

3 cups dry, full-bodied red wine (such as Burgundy, Cabernet Sauvignon, or Malbec)

2 cups low-sodium beef stock

2 bay leaves

6 thyme sprigs

8 slices pancetta (about 3 ounces)

4 small shallots, julienned

12 button mushrooms, trimmed and quartered

CROUTONS

4 slices peasant-style bread

1 garlic clove, halved

2 tablespoons butter

Chopped fresh parsley for garnishing

CONTINUED

Position an oven rack on the middle rung and heat the oven to 300°F.

Using paper towels, pat the short ribs dry. Season them liberally on all sides with salt and pepper. In a Dutch oven or other large, heavy ovenproof pan over medium-high heat, warm the olive oil until shimmering. Add the short ribs, working in batches if necessary to avoid overcrowding the pan, and sear until browned on all sides, about 10 minutes per batch. Using a slotted spoon or tongs, transfer the meat to a plate.

Turn the heat to medium and add the onion, celery, chopped carrots, and smashed garlic to the pan and cook until the vegetables have softened, 5 to 7 minutes. Arrange the short ribs on top of the vegetables, pour in any accumulated juices from the plate, and add the wine, beef stock, bay leaves, and thyme. The meat should be not quite covered by the liquid. Bring everything to a gentle boil, then transfer the pot to the oven to braise until the meat is tender, about 3 hours, stirring and turning the meat once halfway through.

Using a slotted spoon, transfer the meat to a plate. Remove the meat from the bone in chunks, discarding the bones and tendons. Strain and reserve the liquid, discarding the solids.

Wipe out the Dutch oven, and line a plate with a double layer of paper towels.

In the Dutch oven over medium heat, crisp the pancetta in two batches, turning occasionally, about 8 minutes per batch. Transfer to the prepared plate to drain. Add the shallots, mushrooms, and baby carrots to the fat in the pan and cook until golden, about 15 minutes. Add the meat and braising liquid, turn the heat to medium-high and bring to a boil, then lower the heat and simmer for 15 minutes. Taste and season with salt and pepper.

To make the croutons: Rub both sides of the bread slices with the halved garlic. In a large skillet over medium heat, melt the butter until bubbling. Add the bread slices and fry until golden on both sides, about 5 minutes.

Ladle the beef, vegetables, and broth into bowls and garnish with the croutons, crisp pancetta, and parsley. Serve immediately.

"Please don't kill me!" Randolph screamed. He put a hand over his face.

"Just think about the roast beef dinner you'll be eating with Jesus," Andy said. "Why, three seconds from now you'll be spreading your napkin."

The sustained blast from the Kalashnikov rolled Randolph almost all the way to the studio door. Then Andy ran for the rear of the building, ejecting the partially used clip and putting in a full one as he went.

UNDER THE DOME

Roast Beef with Jesus

Makes 6 servings

A bottom round roast comes off the hind leg, just below the rump. It's a well-used muscle, resulting in a flavorful, lean, and tender roast when cooked slowly at a low temperature. Aging it in the refrigerator increases tenderness and flavor; the longer you can leave it in the fridge to age, the more tender and flavorful it will be.

So delicious, it will blow you away.

3- to 4-pound bottom round roast

Kosher salt

Freshly ground black pepper

1 teaspoon Bell's Seasoning or other poultry seasoning

1 tablespoon olive oil

2 cups low-sodium beef stock

1 bay leaf

1 garlic clove, halved

2 tablespoons cornstarch

¼ cup tepid water

2 tablespoons dry sherry

Using paper towels, pat the roast dry. Season it all over with salt and pepper, then with the Bell's. Transfer to the fridge to age, uncovered, for 24 to 72 hours.

About 1 hour before you plan to start cooking, remove the roast from the refrigerator. Position an oven rack on the middle rung and heat the oven to 325°F.

Rub the roast with the olive oil and place it fat-side up on a wire rack in a roasting pan. Pour in the beef stock and add the bay leaf and garlic. Roast until an instant-read thermometer inserted into the thickest part of the meat registers 135°F, 1½ to 1¾ hours, depending on the size of the roast. Transfer the roast to a cutting board and lightly tent with aluminum foil for 15 minutes.

Meanwhile, strain the cooking liquid into a medium saucepan, discarding the bay leaf and garlic. Set the saucepan over medium-high heat and bring this jus to a boil.

In a small bowl, stir together the cornstarch, water, and sherry to form a slurry. When the jus is boiling, remove from the heat, stir in the cornstarch slurry, and then return to the heat. Return to a low boil, stirring occasionally, until this gravy is thickened, about 2 minutes.

Slice the meat thinly and serve, passing the gravy at the table.

Note

Resting a roast allows the juices to return to the center of the meat and results in carryover cooking; the internal temperature of a roast this size will rise about 10°F during a 15-minute rest.

Fish and Shellfish

Billions of years after Maturin the Turtle, suffering from a terrible stomachache, vomited up our universe, the first non-native settlers arrived in Maine to set up fishing stations. From as early as the 1620s, European fishermen came to catch the bountiful cod in the gulf, preserve it in salt, and haul it to the markets back home.

The state's first sardine cannery opened in the mid-1800s, and by 1930, when The Black Spot burned in Derry—that damned cursed town—there were more than fifty canneries up and down the coast, employing thousands. The last sardine cannery closed in 2010, victim to cheaper fish from overseas and people's changing tastes.

One of those changes in tastes was the evolution of lobster from a staple at Shawshank State Prison to a delicacy consumed primarily by the rich. It's hard to imagine Stella Flanders's poor man's soup and the lobster stews and bisques served in New York and Boston as one and the same, but a bit of sherry is really all that stands between them.

These days, Mainers still pluck a fair number of lobsters from the bay, and, of course, there have always been clams. The best place to eat either, or both, is from one of the roadside shacks selling lobster rolls and baskets of steamer clams with brine and butter for dipping. You'll find chowders, too, and the best fish and chips you'll ever taste.

Lobster is expensive everywhere now, even in Maine. Make the most of three lobsters by using the shells to infuse the cream for Poor Man's Soup and then divide the meat between the soup and a half batch of Lobster Pickin's.

While the best place to enjoy them is right here, for those of you from away, you'll find my preferred recipes for fish and shellfish, like the haddock chowder and poached salmon, are gathered mostly from my foremothers. I also owe thanks to my very first boss, from whom I pried (i.e., stole) his top-secret recipe for fish fry mix. He used it to bread clams, but also in his fish batter, along with a bit of milk to help with the browning and an ounce of vodka, which evaporates faster than water, creating a thin, crispy crust.

Fresh is all that most people talk about these days, but I remember the stories my grandmothers told of working in the canneries, and how proud Mainers were of their canned seafood. Canned crab works a treat for the crab canapés—combined with store-bought phyllo cups, it's hard to find an easier recipe for a decadent cocktail-time treat. Fresh snails are hard to come by, at least around here, so the recipe for escargot, another one from my Auntie Mae, uses canned too. Finally, every Mainer I know always has at least one can of evaporated milk on the shelves for the times when there's no cream in the fridge but chowder is on the menu.

Cooking fish and shellfish the Maine way means making the most of what you have, treating your ingredients with respect, and preparing the meal with love.

"What do you think the Rockefellers are eating this evening at their place in Bar Harbor?" she asked indignantly. "What do you think the swells are eating at Twenty-One and Sardi's in New York City? Peanut butter and jelly sandwiches? They're eating lobster, Eddie, same as we are! Now come on—give it a try."

IT

Ellie circulated with a silver tray loaded with canapés, little rolls with a feathered toothpick poked through each one. Her picture of Gage was tucked firmly under her arm.

PET SEMATARY

Crab Canapés

Makes about 40 canapés

Quick and easy to prepare, this simple recipe combines store-bought phyllo cups and the age-old potluck favorite, crab dip, for one-bite hors d'oeuvres that are always a crowd-pleaser, no matter how somber the occasion.

A foolish flatlander might spend extra for fresh lump crabmeat, but most Mainers I know are just fine using pasteurized crab for these delicious crunchy bites. Store leftovers in the refrigerator for up to 2 days. Re-crisp in a 350°F oven for 3 to 4 minutes before serving.

8 ounces cream cheese, at room temperature

1 egg

Grated zest of 1 lemon, plus 2 teaspoons fresh lemon juice

½ teaspoon kosher salt

½ teaspoon Old Bay Seasoning

8 ounces pasteurized or canned crabmeat, lightly squeezed to remove excess moisture

4 green onions, white and light green parts, minced

40 mini phyllo pastry cups

Chopped fresh parsley for garnishing

Position an oven rack on the upper-middle rung and heat the oven to 375°F. Line a baking sheet with parchment paper.

In a medium bowl, using a handheld mixer on medium speed, combine the cream cheese, egg, lemon zest, lemon juice, salt, and Old Bay and beat together until creamy and well combined. Using a spatula or wooden spoon, gently fold in the crabmeat and green onions.

Fill each phyllo cup with 1 to 1½ teaspoons of the crab mixture and set on the prepared baking sheet. Bake until golden, 15 to 20 minutes. Then transfer to a wire rack and let cool for 5 minutes.

Arrange the crab canapés on a platter, garnish with the parsley, and serve warm.

Lobster Pickin's

Makes 6 appetizer servings

Outside of New England and the Atlantic provinces to the north, lobster probably isn't something you'd find on the menu at a middle-of-the-road place like The Lamplighter. Woe is you! Served with Tarragon Tartar Sauce, these are worthy of five stars whether you're in 1958 or 2058.

If you're not up to killing the lobsters yourself, buy fresh or frozen lobster meat, in chunks, from your fishmonger or supermarket. There's no two ways about it, you've got to try these. Otherwise, you'll always wonder—just like Jake Epping.

Vegetable oil for frying
1 cup New England Fry Mix (page 228)
¼ teaspoon garlic powder (optional)
1 cup buttermilk (see "Buttermilk," page 6)
12 to 16 ounces lobster meat (from 3 cold-water lobsters, 1½ to 2 pounds each; see Note, page 101), preferably from Maine
Chopped fresh chives for garnishing
Tarragon Tartar Sauce (page 228) for serving
Smoky Cocktail Sauce (page 229) for serving

Line a baking sheet with a double layer of paper towels. In a Dutch oven or other large, heavy pot over medium-high heat, warm 4 inches of vegetable oil.

In a pie plate, whisk together the fry mix and garlic powder (if using). Pour the buttermilk into a medium bowl. Keep watch on the oil as you proceed with breading the lobster.

Add the lobster meat to the fry mix and toss to coat the pieces evenly. Shake off the excess mix and transfer the lobster pieces to the buttermilk. Mix with your hands to coat each piece, then remove the lobster pieces a few at a time, shaking off the excess liquid, and drop them back into the fry mix. Toss to coat well.

CONTINUED

When the oil reaches 375°F, shake the excess coating from about half of the lobster pieces and gently scatter into the hot oil, keeping them separated so they don't stick together. Fry, untouched, for 30 seconds, then stir gently and continue frying until golden, 1 to 2 minutes more. Using a slotted spoon, transfer the lobster to the prepared baking sheet to drain. Repeat with the remaining lobster.

Arrange the pickin's on a platter, garnish with chives, and serve immediately with the tartar and cocktail sauces.

Vern was licking his lips in a compulsive sort of way, as if he
had tasted some obscure new delicacy, a Howard Johnson's 29th flavor,
Tibetan Sausage Rolls, Interstellar Escargot, something so weird
that it excited and revolted him at the same time.

Teddy only stood and looked. The wind whipped his greasy, clotted
hair first away from his ears and then back over them. His face was
a total blank. I could tell you I saw something there, and perhaps
I did, in hindsight . . . but not then.

"THE BODY"

Interstellar Escargot

Makes 4 appetizer servings

For this manifestation of a boy's imagination, I turned to another one of Auntie Mae's recipes, a Sichuan classic, salt-and-pepper squid. Use the best-quality canned escargot, or snails, you can find, usually from France.

Opening up a can of snails for the first time can be intimidating. More alien than interstellar, if you ask me. So, rekindle that sense of adventure you had as a kid, break out the can opener, and enjoy these little fellas all spiced up.

Vegetable oil for frying, plus 1 tablespoon

One 7-ounce can escargot snails, drained

1 teaspoon kosher salt

½ teaspoon ground white pepper

¼ cup cornstarch

¼ teaspoon baking soda

1 tablespoon butter

1 jalapeño chile, stem removed, minced

½ small red bell pepper, julienned

4 green onions, white and green parts, thinly sliced on the diagonal

2 garlic cloves, minced

¼ teaspoon Chinese 5-spice powder

Chopped fresh cilantro for garnishing

Line a plate with a double layer of paper towels. In a medium saucepan or skillet over medium-high heat, warm ½ inch of vegetable oil.

Pat the snails dry with a paper towel and season with ½ teaspoon of the salt and ¼ teaspoon of the white pepper. In a small bowl, stir together the cornstarch and baking soda. Toss the snails in the cornstarch to coat and then shake off the excess.

CONTINUED

When the oil reaches 350°F, add the snails and fry until golden, about 2 minutes. Using a slotted spoon, transfer the snails to the prepared plate to drain.

In a wok or large skillet over high heat, warm the 1 tablespoon vegetable oil and butter. Add the jalapeño, bell pepper, green onions, and garlic and fry, stirring constantly, until the vegetables have softened, about 90 seconds. Add the snails, remaining ½ teaspoon salt, remaining ¼ teaspoon white pepper, and Chinese 5-spice powder and toss to combine.

Garnish the escargot with cilantro, divide onto plates, and serve.

"Everything I ever wanted or needed was here," she would tell them. "We had the radio and now we have the television, and that's all I want of the world beyond the Reach. I had my garden year in and year out. And lobster? Why, we always used to have a pot of lobster stew on the back of the stove and we used to take it off and put it behind the door in the pantry when the minister came calling so he wouldn't see we were eating 'poor man's soup.'"

"THE REACH"

Poor Man's Soup

Makes 6 servings

This dish is a two-day affair, and I guarantee steeping the lobster shells in cream makes my lobster stew more labor intensive than the one Stella Flanders hid behind her pantry door on Goat Island—but lobsters aren't nineteen cents a pound anymore, and only a fool would let all that flavor go to waste.

Serve with oyster crackers and sweet mixed pickles for a century-old meal from the islands beyond The Reach.

6 tablespoons butter

2 cold-water lobsters (about 1½ pounds each; see Note), preferably from Maine

½ cup dry sherry

3 cups half-and-half or light cream

2 cups whipping cream

Kosher salt

1 to 2 teaspoons fresh lemon juice

Freshly ground black pepper

Chopped fresh chives for garnishing

In a stockpot over medium heat, melt 4 table-spoons of the butter until bubbling. Add the lobster coral, if there is any, stirring to blend. Add the lobster bodies and shells and cook, stirring, until the shells turn a deep red, 5 to 8 minutes.

Add the sherry to the stockpot and boil until almost dry, about 1 minute. Stir in the half-and-half and whipping cream and cook until just simmering, then turn the heat to medium-low and simmer gently, stirring often, until reduced by one-fourth and thickened slightly, about 30 minutes. Do not allow to boil. Stir in 1 tea-spoon salt. Pour into a shallow metal or glass bowl, set on top of a wire rack or trivet, and stir occasionally to cool quickly and completely. Cover and refrigerate overnight.

The next day, strain the cream, discarding the bodies and solids.

In a large pot over medium heat, melt the remaining 2 tablespoons butter until bubbling. Add the reserved lobster meat and cook until warmed through, 3 to 5 minutes. Slowly pour the strained cream mixture over the lobster and cook until steaming, 7 to 10 minutes more. Add 1 teaspoon of the lemon juice; taste and season with salt, pepper, and more lemon if needed.

Divide the lobster meat and soup among bowls, garnish with chives, and serve.

Note

To prepare the lobsters, bring a large pot of generously salted water to a boil. Put the lobsters in the freezer until they are dormant (no longer react or move when handled), 5 to 15 minutes. Prepare an ice bath by filling a large bowl (or bucket) with ice and cold water.

Set one lobster on a clean, folded dish towel on top of a cutting board. Place the tip of a large knife over the center of the head, at the first joint behind the eyes, blade facing forward. Quickly and forcefully drive the knife down through the head to the cutting board, then follow through, bringing the knife down and slicing between the eyes. Repeat with the remaining lobster.

Cut the elastics from their claws and plunge the lobsters into the boiling water until just cooked through, about 4 minutes. Using tongs, transfer the lobsters to the prepared ice bath until completely cool. Wash and dry the pot.

Twist the claws, tails, and legs from the bodies. Reserve the coral (eggs) if there is any, but discard the tomalley (liver); set the bodies aside. The tomalley of lobsters can contain high levels of toxins and is best discarded.

Crack the tails and claws, and remove all the meat, keeping the claw meat as intact as possible. Remove the meat from the legs by crushing the shell of each at one end with a rolling pin, and continue rolling up the length of the leg, squeezing the meat from the tube of the shell, like toothpaste. Reserve all the shells.

Keep the claw meat intact; chop the remaining meat into large chunks. Cover, and store in the fridge overnight.

A week or so after that, Richie got the kid to start heating his beer on the stove. Can you feature that? The kid all by himself in that apartment with his dad turning into . . . well, into something . . . an' heating his beer and then having to listen to him—it—drinking it with awful thick slurping sounds, the way an old man eats his chowder: Can you imagine it?

"GRAY MATTER"

Haddock Chowdah for Old Men

Makes 6 servings

An old-fashioned, East Coast chowder flavored with salt pork and ale and thickened just before serving. Choose a pale or amber ale that is low in hops, which turn bitter when cooked—I don't want to imagine what that cheap swill Richie Grenadine drank tasted like warm.

Serve with saltines, common crackers, or the cheese biscuits from Sausage on Cheese Biscuits to Go (page 27).

2-inch cube salt pork, diced

1 medium yellow onion, julienned

2 celery stalks, chopped

1 cup pale or amber ale

1 large russet potato, peeled and cut into bite-size wedges

2 bay leaves

1 thyme sprig

4 cups water

2 cups half-and-half or light cream (see Note)

12 ounces haddock or other white fish (such as cod or halibut), cut into 2-inch pieces

Kosher salt

Ground white pepper

2 tablespoons all-purpose flour

2 tablespoons butter, at room temperature

Line a small plate with a double layer of paper towels.

Put the salt pork in a cold Dutch oven or large saucepan, set over medium heat, and render the fat from the pork, stirring occasionally and lowering the heat as necessary to prevent burning. When the pork is crisp, scoop it from the pan with a slotted spoon and transfer to the prepared plate to drain. Pour off all but 2 tablespoons of fat from the pan.

Turn the heat to medium-high, add the onion and celery to the fat in the pan, and cook, stirring occasionally, until soft and translucent, about 5 minutes. Stir in the ale, potato, bay leaves, and thyme. When the liquid has reduced and the pot is almost dry, add the water and bring to a boil. Then turn the heat to medium-low, partially cover, and simmer until the potato is tender, about 20 minutes.

Add the half-and-half, fish, 1 teaspoon salt, and ½ teaspoon white pepper to the pan and cook gently until piping hot and steaming, but do not allow to boil. Then remove from the heat, cover the pot, and allow to stand for 1 hour to give the flavor time to deepen.

In a small bowl, using a fork, mash together the flour and butter until combined into a paste.

Reheat the soup over medium heat until steaming. Stir in the butter-flour mixture and cook until the starch has cooked off and the chowder is glossy and slightly thickened, about 7 minutes. Do not boil. Taste and season with additional salt and white pepper. Remove and discard the bay leaves and thyme.

Divide the chowder into bowls, garnish with the crisp salt pork, and serve piping hot.

Note
No cream? Substitute two 12-ounce cans evaporated milk.

Because of my preparations for the following day, I dropped by The
Lamplighter for my evening beer later than usual, but there was no
risk of encountering Frank Dunning. It was his day to take his kids
to the football game in Orono, and on the way back they were going to
stop at the Ninety-Fiver for fried clams and milkshakes.

11/22/63

Fried Clam Rolls

Makes 4 servings

NOTHING can replace the taste of fresh soft-shelled Ipswich clams, raked from the tidal flats, shucked, and served up fresh the same day. Whole-bellied buggers are what you want, no clam strips for this born-and-bred Mainer, thank you very much.

I've heard a few visitors from California claim that large Manila clams from the West Coast make a decent clam roll when fried right, but as for myself, I'll never know.

1 pound fresh Ipswich clams, shucked and siphons trimmed

One 12-ounce can evaporated milk

1 teaspoon hot sauce (such as Louisiana or Tabasco)

Vegetable oil or vegetable shortening for frying

4 hot dog buns (preferably split-top)

2 tablespoons butter, melted

2 cups New England Fry Mix (page 228)

Tarragon Tartar Sauce (page 228) for spreading

Lemon wedges for squeezing

Rinse the clams in lots of fresh water to remove any mud or grit. In a large bowl, combine the clams, evaporated milk, and hot sauce; let soak for 30 minutes.

Position an oven rack on the middle rung and heat the oven to 250°F. Line a plate with two layers of paper towels. In a Dutch oven or other large, heavy pot over medium-high heat, warm 4 inches of vegetable oil. Keep watch on the oil as you proceed to prepare the rest of the ingredients.

Set a skillet over medium-high heat. Brush the tops and bottoms of the hot dog buns with the melted butter, place in the skillet, and fry, turning once, until both buttered sides are golden, about 3 minutes. Move the toasted buns to a plate and put in the oven to keep warm.

CONTINUED

Pour the fry mix into a baking dish. By the handful, remove the clams from the milk, shaking off the excess liquid, and drop them into the fry mix. Toss well to ensure all the clams are coated evenly.

When the oil has reached 375°F, carefully add the clams, one or two handfuls at a time so they don't stick together, and fry, untouched, for 30 seconds. Stir gently and continue frying until golden, 1 to 2 minutes more. Using a slotted spoon, transfer the clams to the prepared plate to drain and then move them to an ovenproof plate and put into the oven to keep warm. Repeat with the remaining clams.

Spread tartar sauce on the inside of the grilled buns, pile the fried clams on top, and serve immediately with lemon wedges for squeezing.

"Nah, God just told me I needed a hamburger at the Village Cafe," I
said. "Or maybe it was His opposite number. Please say Buddy's still
doing business at the same old stand."

She smiled. It warmed her face back up again, and I was happy to see
it. "He'll still be there when Ki's kids are old enough to try buying
beer with fake IDs. Unless someone wanders in off the road and asks
for something like shrimp tetrazzini. If that happened, he'd probably
drop dead of a heart attack."

BAG OF BONES

Shrimp Tetrazzini

Makes 4 servings

Good things come from dark places. This recipe came on a scrap of newspaper in a box in Mama's dugout basement. Page 14 of the *Kansas City* (MO) *Star*, November 21, 1920: "The famous singer is so fond of spaghetti that she brought a recipe from her home in Italy. Rumor has it that Tetrazzini eats freely of her favorite dish and can prepare it herself, if need be, from this recipe."

Some people use turkey, others chicken, but I like my play on Luisa Tetrazzini's recipe best. The fresh shrimp, pine nuts, tomatoes, sherry, and cream would have had Buddy Jellison keeling over dead right next to his deep-fat fryer.

12 large shrimp, peeled and deveined

3 tablespoons olive oil

Kosher salt

Freshly ground black pepper

½ teaspoon sweet paprika

8 ounces dried spaghettini or angel hair pasta

1 small yellow onion, finely chopped

2 small, ripe Roma tomatoes, cored, seeded, and finely chopped

1 garlic clove, finely grated or minced

½ cup dry sherry

1 cup whipping cream

¼ cup fresh or frozen green peas

1 cup grated Parmesan cheese, plus more for serving

¼ cup pine nuts

1 tablespoon chopped fresh oregano or parsley

Bring a large pot of generously salted water to a boil. In a small bowl, toss the shrimp with 1 tablespoon of the olive oil, ½ teaspoon salt, ¼ teaspoon pepper, and the paprika.

Add the spaghettini to the boiling water and cook until al dente, 8 to 10 minutes. Drain, and cover to keep warm.

CONTINUED

Position an oven rack on a rung 6 inches below the top element and heat the oven's broiler (set to low, if possible).

In a large, deep, ovenproof skillet over medium heat, warm the remaining 2 tablespoons olive oil until shimmering. Add the onion and cook, stirring occasionally, until soft and translucent, 3 to 5 minutes. Add the tomatoes and cook until softened and dry, about 3 minutes. Turn the heat to high, add the garlic, and stir until fragrant, about 30 seconds. Add the sherry and deglaze the pan by scraping up the browned bits with a wooden spoon, then reduce the liquid until the pan is almost dry, about 1 minute. Pour in the cream, bring to a simmer, and then stir in the peas and ½ cup of the Parmesan. Taste and season with salt and pepper.

Add the pasta to the sauce and toss to coat. Arrange the shrimp on top, transfer the skillet to the oven, and broil until the shrimp are pink, about 3 minutes. Flip the shrimp, then scatter the remaining ½ cup Parmesan and the pine nuts across the top. Return the skillet to the oven and broil until the shrimp are cooked through, the pine nuts are toasted, the cheese is golden, and some of the pasta is crisp, 2 to 3 minutes more. Remove from the oven and sprinkle with the oregano.

Divide the pasta and shrimp among plates and serve immediately, passing more Parmesan at the table.

She had bought some lovely fillet of sole, thinking she would pan-broil it if they decided to stay overnight. Sole was good because Gerald, who would live on a diet of nothing but roast beef and fried chicken if left to his own devices (with the occasional order of deep-fried mushrooms thrown in for nutritional purposes), actually claimed to like sole. She had bought it without the slightest premonition that he would be eaten before he could eat.

GERALD'S GAME

Pan-Broiled Sole with Lime

Makes 4 servings

Going upta camp to work out the kinks with a game or two? Buy some fresh fish along the way and make this quick and easy dish with a flavorful lime dressing spiked with cilantro, garlic, and fish sauce. Steam some rice, toss a green salad, and you'll have dinner on the table in 30 minutes, once you can find someone to uncuff you from the bed, that is. I shouldn't make fun. But the pickles some people get themselves into! Can't find sole? Try boneless fillets of flounder, haddock, or tilapia instead.

2 to 3 limes

3 tablespoons Asian fish sauce

2 tablespoons light brown sugar

2 tablespoons finely chopped fresh cilantro or parsley

4 garlic cloves, finely grated or minced

½ teaspoon red pepper flakes

4 skinless sole fillets

Kosher salt

Freshly ground black pepper

½ cup all-purpose flour

4 tablespoons vegetable oil

1 small red chile, thinly sliced on the diagonal

Zest one of the limes by grating it on a kitchen rasp/Microplane. (Avoid grating the white pith, which is bitter.) Juice the lime to produce 2 tablespoons juice, using another lime for juice if needed. Slice the remaining lime into wedges for serving.

In a small saucepan over high heat, combine the fish sauce and brown sugar and stir until the sugar dissolves, about 1 minute. Remove the pan from the heat and stir in the lime zest, lime juice, cilantro, garlic, and red pepper flakes. Partially cover to keep warm.

Lightly season the sole with salt and black pepper on both sides. Pour the flour onto a large plate and lightly dredge the sole fillets, turning to coat; shake off the excess flour.

In a large pan over medium-high heat, warm 2 tablespoons of the vegetable oil until shimmering. Arrange two fillets in the pan and cook until lightly browned, turning once, 1 to 2 minutes per side. Transfer to plates, wipe out the skillet, and repeat with the remaining 2 tablespoons vegetable oil and sole.

Drizzle the lime sauce over each fillet, garnish with the red chile, and serve immediately, passing the lime wedges at the table.

But now they have cancelled the fireworks . . . and no matter what anyone says, Marty feels that it is really the Fourth itself—his Fourth—that they have done to death.

Only his Uncle Al, who blew into town late this morning to have the traditional salmon and fresh peas with the family, had understood. He had listened closely, standing on the verandah tiles in his dripping bathing suit (the others were swimming and laughing in the Coslaws' new pool on the other side of the house) after lunch.

THE CYCLE OF THE WEREWOLF

Poached Salmon for the Fourth

Makes 4 servings

Locals have been feasting on salmon and peas since long before we drew state and national boundaries. The fish migrating up our rivers from the Atlantic provide much-needed fresh protein, and our gardens provide freshly shucked peas, as well as new potatoes, rounding out an early-summer meal celebrating the natural abundance and cycle of the land.

The egg sauce is a modern version of the traditional sauce of cream and hard-boiled eggs that my grannie's grandmother served with her poached salmon.

POACHED SALMON

4 salmon fillets (6 ounces each), skin removed

Kosher salt

½ cup dry white wine

½ cup water

1 large shallot, sliced lengthwise

1 garlic clove, smashed

2 parsley sprigs

2 dill sprigs (optional)

2 slices lemon

EGG SAUCE

¼ cup butter

1 large shallot, minced

2 tablespoons all-purpose flour

½ cup dry white wine

½ cup poaching liquid reserved from salmon

1 cup whipping cream

2 hard-boiled eggs (see Note), chopped

2 tablespoons chopped fresh chives

1 teaspoon fresh lemon juice

1 pinch cayenne pepper

Kosher salt

Lemon wedges for squeezing

CONTINUED

Fish and Shellfish

To poach the salmon: Position an oven rack on the middle rung and heat the oven to 250°F.

Lightly season the salmon with salt.

In a large skillet, combine the wine, water, shallot, and garlic. Lay the parsley, dill (if using), and lemon slices in the middle of the pan to make a bed for the salmon. Set the pan over medium heat and bring to a simmer. Lay the fillets on top of the bed, cover, turn the heat to medium-low, and simmer until the flesh flakes with a fork but is still medium-rare in the center, about 5 minutes for fillets that are ½ inch thick. Transfer the salmon to an ovenproof plate, tent lightly with aluminum foil, and keep warm in the oven. Reserve ½ cup of the poaching liquid.

To make the egg sauce: While the salmon cooks, in a medium saucepan over medium-high heat, melt the butter until bubbling. Add the shallot and sauté until softened and just turning golden, about 3 minutes. Sprinkle in the flour, stir until combined, and remove the pan from the heat.

When the salmon is in the oven, return the saucepan to medium-high heat, stir in the wine and reserved poaching liquid, and boil, stirring continuously, until slightly reduced, about 3 minutes. Stir in the cream and boil, stirring occasionally, until reduced enough to coat the back of a spoon, 4 to 5 minutes more. Stir in the eggs, 1 tablespoon of the chives, the lemon juice, and cayenne. Taste and season with salt. Transfer the sauce to a gravy boat and garnish with the remaining 1 tablespoon chives.

Divide the salmon fillets onto plates and serve immediately with lemon wedges for squeezing, passing the sauce at the table.

Note

To hard-boil eggs, gently place them in a saucepan with enough water to cover by 1 inch. Set over high heat and bring to a boil. Remove from the heat, cover, and let stand for 10 minutes. Drain and cover with cold water to cool. When the water warms, drain and replace it with cold water; repeat until the eggs have cooled completely. Store hard-boiled eggs in the fridge for up to 1 week.

"'I'm no Sherlock Holmes, Doc,' I says, 'but I can go you one better than that.'

"'Really?' he says, kinda skeptical.

"'Ayuh,' I says. 'I think he had his supper either at Curly's or Jan's Wharfside over here, or Yanko's on Moose-Look.'

"'Why one of those, when there's got to be fifty restaurants within a twenty-mile radius of where we're standin that sell fish dinners, even in April?' he asks. 'Why not the Grey Gull, for that matter?'

"'Because the Grey Gull would not stoop to selling fish and chips,' I says, 'and that's what this guy had.'"

THE COLORADO KID

Moose-Lickit Fish and Chips

Makes 4 servings

Those born and bred on the islands are a breed beyond even us mainland Mainers. Life on the coast is hard enough, but those surrounded by water on all sides face the harsh storms of winter, followed by gales of tourists in the spring and summer. Island life will never be for the faint of heart, including me.

The recipes for the fry mix and batter come from an island fish shack off Freeport, where I worked my first summer after high school, when getting out of Pownal was all that mattered. One season was enough—I came back home and never left again.

Four 6-ounce pieces white fish (such as cod, haddock, or pollock), skin removed

1 teaspoon kosher salt

1 cup New England Fry Mix (page 228)

2 teaspoons baking powder

¾ cup milk, or as needed

¼ cup vodka or water

1 egg

1 recipe Garlic Fries (page 163; blanched, but not yet fried) and garlic sauce (optional)

Vegetable oil for frying

Tarragon Tartar Sauce (page 228) for serving

Lemon wedges for squeezing

Position an oven rack on the middle rung and heat the oven to 250°F. Line a large ovenproof bowl with a double layer of paper towels. Line a baking sheet with paper towels.

Using paper towels, pat the fish dry and season with the salt.

CONTINUED

In a large bowl, whisk together the fry mix and baking powder. Coat the fish pieces in this mixture, shake off the excess, and set aside on a plate.

Add the milk, vodka, and egg to the fry mix, and whisk well to combine. Let this batter stand for 25 minutes.

Meanwhile, pour the fries into a Dutch oven and add enough vegetable oil to just cover. Set over high heat and cook, stirring once at 2 minutes and again at 7 minutes. The fries become a bit fragile at this stage, so allow them to cook untouched until they begin to crisp, 12 to 15 minutes. Continue to cook, stirring occasionally, until they are crisp on the outside and tender on the inside, 18 to 22 minutes more, depending on the thickness of the fries.

Using a slotted spoon, remove the fries from the oil and transfer to the prepared bowl to drain. Then discard the paper towels and put the bowl into the oven to keep the fries warm, reserving the garlic sauce (if using). Remove the fry oil from the heat temporarily.

Whisk the batter to recombine, adding milk, 1 tablespoon at a time, to thin to the consistency of pancake batter, if necessary. Reheat the oil over high heat until an instant-read thermometer registers 350°F.

Dip a piece of fish in the batter to coat, and gently shake off any excess. Carefully lay the fish in the oil and repeat with the remaining pieces, frying in two batches, if necessary, to avoid overcrowding the pan. Cook, turning occasionally, until golden brown, 5 to 6 minutes.

Using the slotted spoon, remove the fish from the oil and transfer to the prepared baking sheet to drain. Toss the fries with the garlic sauce, if desired.

Divide the fish and chips among plates and serve immediately with tartar sauce and lemon wedges for squeezing.

Vegetarian

In the beginning, there were beans, corn, and squash. Maine's early settlers depended upon the traditional trinity of Native American cuisine to survive, and we still eat them today as corn chowder, baked beans, roasted summer squash, and other down-home dishes.

Alongside, there was meat if you could afford it, or at least the ammunition to shoot it yourself. Men like my granddaddy were always out hunting for the family; to them, the very ideas of meatless chili and baked beans without pork would have sounded straight from the land of make-believe.

There sure weren't many who thought two women could make a go of it with a vegetarian Mexican restaurant in Portland, never mind Castle Rock, but the town has come a long way since the days of that evil Leland Gaunt and his shop of Needful Things; for as long as Missy and Deirdre owned Holy Frijole, it was a rare Saturday night when there was a table open or space at the bar before closing.

Missy's recipes taught me a lot about cooking without meat. For instance, refined coconut oil is a good substitute for the lard in refried beans. If you don't have it on hand, you can replace it with olive oil or vegetable oil, but coconut oil is solid at room temperature, like lard, and its smoke point is high at 400°F, so it's good to have on hand for frying. I've been told it makes a good moisturizer too.

The comfort food that Missy cooked at home was just as flavor-packed. Her curried millet and summer squash casserole is a substantial main, packed with taste as well as nutrition thanks to the peanut sauce drizzled across the top just before serving. Her recipe for homemade pasta is the best I've yet to find, and makes whipping up fresh fettuccini on a weeknight quick and easy.

It was Missy who inspired me to take the salt pork out of Dick Hallorann's baked beans, which I know will upset a few folks, but he always added a spoonful of tomato paste and a good dose of Maine maple syrup before he put them in the pot, and I swear to you the flavor in these beans means you won't miss a thing.

Most Mainers' favorite thing about bean suppers is the leftovers. I used to pack cold bean sandwiches on white bread spread with mayonnaise and mustard for Ray when he went off foraging or fishing after the squads took his dad. When he came back with wild mushrooms in the fall, I turned out batches of pies, freezing them unbaked for quick dinners throughout the coming winter. They cook up golden from frozen—brush them with egg wash just before putting them in the oven, and add a few minutes to the baking time.

I didn't used to believe it was possible, especially with all the hunters around here, but over the years, because of circumstance rather than choice, I've discovered tricks and tips to cooking without meat that satisfy the most committed carnivores.

Not every day, mind, let's not get crazy. One meal at a time.

You're not going to drink my blood, are you?
Like a vampire?

The thing in the bed smiles without smiling.
We are, so far as I can express it in your terms,
vegetarians.

Yeah, but what about Bowser there? Jonesy points
to the legless weasel, and it bares a mouthful
of needle teeth in a grotesque grin. *Is Bowser*
a vegetarian?

DREAMCATCHER

"Danforth?" Myrtle asked suddenly. "Could you let me out at Amanda Williams's house? I know it's a little out of the way, but she's got my fondue pot. I thought—" The shy smile came and went on her face again. "I thought I might make you—*us*—a little treat. For the football game. . . ."

He opened his mouth to tell her the Williamses' was a *lot* out of his way, the game was about to start, and she could get her goddam fondue pot tomorrow. He didn't like cheese when it was hot and runny anyway. . . .

NEEDFUL THINGS

GameDay Fondue

Makes 4 servings

It's no surprise Danforth Keeton hated fondue. Contrary to that miserable old codger's disagreeable character, it is a sociable dish meant to gather family and friends around the table.

This version of the Swiss national dish is a balance of American and European, using beer, bourbon, Old Bay, Gruyère, Dijon, and the secret that keeps it all smooth and blended, Babybel cheese—just don't forget to unwrap them.

2 tablespoons bourbon

1 tablespoon cornstarch

½ teaspoon Old Bay Seasoning

⅛ teaspoon baking soda

Kosher salt

1 cup Pilsner beer, or as needed

1 garlic clove, minced or grated

1 cup grated Gruyère cheese

6 mini Babybel Original cheese rounds, shredded

2 teaspoons Dijon mustard

1 to 2 teaspoons fresh lemon juice

1 day-old French baguette, or 4 soft pretzels, cut into 1-inch cubes

Pickles, raw vegetables, roasted mushrooms, grilled sausage, and/or chunks of ham for dipping

In a small bowl, whisk together the bourbon and cornstarch until smooth. In another small bowl, combine the Old Bay, baking soda, and ½ teaspoon salt. Prepare a fondue pot and fill the fuel burner as directed.

CONTINUED

Vegetarian

In a medium saucepan over medium-high heat, combine the beer and garlic and bring to a boil. Remove the pan from the heat, stir the bourbon and cornstarch to recombine, and then whisk into the beer. Return the saucepan to medium-high heat and simmer briskly until thickened, 3 to 5 minutes. Turn the heat to low and gradually add both cheeses in three additions, whisking until smooth and fully incorporated between each addition.

Stir in the Old Bay mix, Dijon, and 1 teaspoon of the lemon juice. Taste and adjust the lemon juice and salt if necessary. Transfer to the prepared fondue pot and light the burner.

Serve the fondue immediately with the baguette, pickles, vegetables, mushrooms, sausage, and/or ham. Instruct guests to dip their forks and swirl in a figure-8 pattern to keep the fondue from setting or clumping. (If the fondue thickens, thin with 1 tablespoon of beer and whisk until smooth.)

After he had finished checking over the salads his understudy had made
and peeked in on the home-baked beans they were using as appetizers
this week, Halloran untied his apron, hung it on a hook, and slipped
out the back door. He had maybe forty-five minutes before he had to
crank up for dinner in earnest.

The name of this place was the Red Arrow Lodge, and it was buried
in the western Maine mountains, thirty miles from the town of Rangely.
It was a good gig, Halloran thought. . . .

THE SHINING

Dick Hallorann's Baked Beans

Makes 8 servings

I'll never understand why Dick Hallorann, after barely surviving that fire at The Black Spot when he was nineteen, came back to Maine. But he did, year after year; I have his original bean recipe from Red Arrow Lodge to prove it. He used one part salt pork, by weight, with two parts dried beans; he scored the rind and buried the pork under the beans along with the onion.

I've eliminated the pork here, but I still use his heavy hand with the pepper to counter gas; not sure it works, but I do know peppery beans taste best.

3 cups large dried beans (such as Marfax, yellow eye, or kidney; see "Beans," page 6, and Notes)
1 tablespoon kosher salt, plus 1 teaspoon
½ cup molasses
¼ cup maple syrup
2 tablespoons apple cider vinegar
1 tablespoon tomato paste
1 tablespoon mustard powder
1 teaspoon freshly ground black pepper
1 small yellow onion, halved
1 bay leaf
About 4 cups boiling water

Rinse the dried beans and, in a large bowl, combine them with enough warm water to cover by 4 inches. Cover with a clean dish towel and leave on the counter overnight. Drain the beans.

In a medium saucepan over high heat, combine the beans with enough water to cover by 1 inch. Add the 1 tablespoon salt, bring to a boil, and maintain a low boil for 10 minutes. Lower the heat to a simmer, partially cover, and cook until the beans are tender and the skins burst when you blow on a spoonful of them, 20 to 30 minutes. Drain.

CONTINUED

DICK HALLORANN'S BAKED BEANS, CONTINUED

Position an oven rack on the bottom rung and heat the oven to 250°F.

In a large bean pot or Dutch oven, combine the beans, remaining 1 teaspoon salt, molasses, maple syrup, vinegar, tomato paste, mustard powder, and pepper and stir well. Bury the onion and bay leaf beneath the beans and add just enough of the boiling water to cover. Cover and bake until tender, 3 to 4 hours, checking occasionally to ensure the beans are not dry. Keep adding just enough boiling water to cover if necessary.

Transfer the pot of beans to a wire rack or trivet, discard the bay leaf, and serve piping hot.

Notes

Dried kidney beans contain a toxic protein called phytohemagglutinin that can cause gastrointestinal distress. They must be boiled for 10 minutes to destroy it.

If your dried beans have been in your pantry for more than six months, add ½ teaspoon baking soda to the soaking water to help them soften. Rinse well before proceeding with the recipe.

"Dead zone?"

"It's like some of the signals don't conduct," Johnny said. "I can never get streets or addresses. Numbers are hard but they sometimes come." The waitress returned with Johnny's tea and chili. He tasted the chili and nodded at Bannerman. "You're right. It's good. Especially on a night like this."

"Go to it," Bannerman said. "Man, I love good chili. My ulcer hollers bloody hell about it. Fuck you, ulcer, I say. Down the hatch."

———

THE DEAD ZONE

Vegan Chili at Jon's

Makes 6 servings

Jon's Restaurant was located in Bridgton, a town not far from Castle Rock with its own terrifying history. Jon's served down-to-earth, home-cooked food. He wouldn't have been caught dead with meatless chili on his menu, but the Rock saw big changes when they rebuilt. Time marches on, and food with it. Store leftover chili in an airtight container in the refrigerator for up to 5 days, or in the freezer for up to 4 weeks.

2 tablespoons olive oil

12 ounces vegan ground round (see Note)

1 large white onion, julienned

2 celery stalks, diced

Kosher salt

4 garlic cloves, finely grated or minced

2 tablespoons tomato paste

2 tablespoons chili powder

2 teaspoons ground cumin

1 teaspoon dried oregano

One 28-ounce can whole tomatoes, with juices

One 15-ounce can black beans, drained and rinsed

One 15-ounce can kidney beans, drained and rinsed

1 cup water

2 chipotle chiles in adobo sauce, minced

2 teaspoons fresh lime juice

Freshly ground black pepper

Warmed corn tortillas (see page 230), chopped cilantro, sliced avocado, diced tomato, thinly sliced white onion, and/or shredded vegan cheese for garnishing

In a Dutch oven or other large, heavy pot over high heat, warm the olive oil until shimmering. Add the vegan ground round and cook, breaking it up with a wooden spoon, until it is sizzling and the fat has rendered, 3 to 5 minutes. Add the onion, celery, and ½ teaspoon salt and cook, stirring occasionally, until soft, 5 to 7 minutes. Add the garlic, tomato paste, chili powder, cumin, and oregano and cook, stirring constantly, until fragrant, about 1 minute more.

Add the canned tomatoes and their juices, black beans, kidney beans, water, and chipotles to the pot. Stir to combine, turn the heat to medium-high, and bring to a low boil. Then turn the heat to medium-low and simmer, stirring occasionally, for 45 minutes. Remove the chili from the heat and stir in the lime juice. Taste and season with salt and pepper.

Serve the chili piping hot, garnished with your choice of toppings.

Note

If you can't stand the very idea of meatless chili, substitute 1 pound of ground beef for the vegan ground round and then drain most of the fat from the pan before you add the onion and celery.

Full of the caff's version of fettuccini Alfredo, he took a nap and awoke feeling marginally better. He went looking for Maureen and spied her in the formerly deserted East Wing. It seemed the Institute might soon be hosting more guests. He walked down to her and asked if she needed help. "Because I wouldn't mind earning some tokens," he said.

THE INSTITUTE

Fettuccini Alfredo

Makes 4 servings

A staple in restaurants and cafeterias across the globe, fettuccini Alfredo exploded in the late twentieth century into a thousand variations, most of which have little to do with the dish's beginnings as humble Roman home cooking. I can't imagine what those bastards served to the kids they tortured deep in the woods, but the version the diner in Pownal served was bad enough.

This traditional recipe takes the dish back to its simple roots, using butter, Parmesan, and the pasta cooking water to make a rich, silky sauce without cream.

20 ounces fresh fettuccini (see page 232), or 16 ounces dried fettuccini

6 tablespoons butter

1 cup grated Parmesan cheese, plus more for serving

Kosher salt

Freshly ground black pepper

Position an oven rack on the middle rung, set four ovenproof bowls on it, and heat to 250°F. Bring a large pot of generously salted water to a boil.

Add the fettuccini to the boiling water and simmer briskly until al dente; about 3 minutes for fresh pasta, or using the package directions for dried.

Drain the pasta, reserving 2 cups of the cooking water. Return the pasta to the pot and, off the heat, stir in the butter until melted. Gradually add the Parmesan, one small handful at a time, stirring quickly to create an emulsion with the butter. Add the cooking water, as needed, to create a smooth sauce that coats the back of a spoon. Taste and season with salt.

Divide the pasta among the warm bowls and serve immediately, passing pepper and additional Parmesan at the table.

Nettie's Rolled Lasagna

Makes 8 servings

Nettie Cobb's recipe for lasagna called for canned mushrooms, which I will never bring myself to serve, even to an evil old sod like Leland Gaunt. He may have left Castle Rock in ashes, but no soul on earth should have to eat canned mushrooms.

Beside changing to fresh fungus, I also chose to roll the lasagna rather than stack it. There's nothing wrong with trying something new, especially when all around you is flattened to rubble.

3 tablespoons olive oil

8 ounces button mushrooms, sliced

1 small yellow onion, chopped

1½ teaspoons kosher salt

2 teaspoons chopped fresh oregano, or ½ teaspoon dried

3 cups Italian Red Sauce (page 229)

One 10-ounce package frozen chopped spinach, thawed

16 ounces ricotta cheese

1 egg

⅔ cup grated Parmesan cheese

½ teaspoon freshly ground black pepper

8 sheets fresh lasagna, about 3½ by 10 inches (see page 232), uncooked (see Note)

About 1 cup shredded fresh mozzarella cheese

¼ cup roughly torn fresh basil leaves (see Note)

In a medium skillet over medium-high heat, warm the olive oil until shimmering. Add the mushrooms, onion, and ½ teaspoon of the salt and cook, stirring occasionally, until the mushrooms have released their liquid and the onion is golden brown, 8 to 10 minutes. Stir in the oregano, then transfer to a plate and let cool slightly.

CONTINUED

Position an oven rack on the upper-middle rung and heat the oven to 375°F. Cover the center of a 9 by 13-inch baking dish with a thin layer of the red sauce.

Place the thawed spinach in a mound in the middle of a clean dish towel. Roll up the towel and, standing over the sink, wring as much water from the spinach as you can. In a medium bowl, combine the spinach, onion-mushroom mixture, ricotta, egg, ⅓ cup of the Parmesan, remaining 1 teaspoon salt, and pepper and stir to mix.

Spread about 3 tablespoons of the spinach mixture onto the end of a sheet of lasagna. Starting at a short end, roll into a tight spiral, and arrange vertically (so the spirals are visible) on top of the sauce in the baking dish. Repeat with the remaining spinach mixture and lasagna sheets, nesting the rolls in the center of the baking dish, but leaving ¼ inch between them.

Spoon the remaining red sauce over the rolls and top with the mozzarella and remaining ⅓ cup Parmesan. Bake until bubbling and brown, 30 to 35 minutes. Remove from the oven and let rest on a wire rack for 10 minutes.

Divide the lasagna rolls among plates, garnish with the torn basil, and serve.

Notes

If you prefer to use dried lasagna, cook according to package directions, drain, and toss the noodles with 1 teaspoon olive oil before stacking them under a clean dish towel.

Basil blackens shortly after being cut with a metal knife or scissors. Instead of cutting, tear each leaf into three or four pieces to keep its vibrant green color. Gently pack the torn leaves into the measuring cup without crushing them.

Wild Mushroom Hand Pies

Makes 6 hand pies

I imagine Sara Tidwell foraging for wild mushrooms in the woods surrounding her home, Sara Laughs, and returning to the warmth of her kitchen to turn them into these savory hand pies with cornmeal crust. She was a frugal woman, who used the egg white left over from making the pastry to wash the pies just before they went into the oven, for shiny, golden crusts.

They say there's a thinny, a tear in space where realities cross, behind Sara Laughs. Maybe that's what drove Sara mad in the end, though there's not many would blame her, after what they did to her boy.

2 tablespoons butter

2 tablespoons olive oil

3 small shallots, minced

8 ounces wild mushrooms (such as chanterelle, black trumpet, and lobster), trimmed and sliced (see Note)

8 ounces domesticated mushrooms (such as button, shiitake, and oyster), trimmed and sliced

1½ teaspoons kosher salt

½ teaspoon freshly ground black pepper

½ cup dry white wine or dry vermouth

¾ cup cream cheese, at room temperature

1 teaspoon fresh thyme leaves

1 batch Cornmeal–Cream Cheese Pastry (page 139)

1 egg white, whisked with 1 teaspoon water

In a large skillet over medium-high heat, warm the butter and olive oil until bubbling. Add the shallots and cook, stirring occasionally, until soft and just golden, about 10 minutes. Add all the mushrooms, salt, and pepper and cook until the mushrooms have released their liquid and are starting to brown, 12 to 15 minutes. Add the wine and deglaze the pan by scraping up the browned bits with a wooden spoon, then reduce the liquid until the pan is almost dry.

CONTINUED

Vegetarian

Remove the pan from the heat and stir in the cream cheese and thyme until the cheese is melted and this filling is creamy. Pour into a shallow metal bowl or plate, set on top of a wire rack or trivet, and stir occasionally to cool quickly.

Position an oven rack on the lower-middle rung and heat the oven to 375°F. Line a baking sheet with parchment paper.

On a lightly floured work surface, using a rolling pin and even pressure, roll one pastry disc out from the center in all four compass directions: north, south, east, and west. Turn and loosen the dough occasionally as you continue to roll it out into a 12-inch circle that is an even ⅛ inch thick. Repeat with the remaining pastry disc.

Using a pot lid or an inverted bowl as a template, cut out three 6-inch circles from the dough; gently roll each into a slight oblong. Place ⅓ cup of the filling on the bottom half of each oblong. Dampen your fingertip with water and run it around the edge on the half of the dough with no filling. Fold the top over the bottom and seal firmly with your fingertips, gently pressing the dough around the filling to remove any air pockets. Using your fingers or a fork, crimp the edge. Repeat with the remaining dough and filling to make six pies.

Arrange the pies on the prepared baking sheet, brush with the whisked egg white, and bake until light golden, 35 to 40 minutes. Transfer to a wire rack and let cool for 15 minutes.

Serve the hand pies warm or at room temperature.

Note

No fresh wild mushrooms? Soak ½ ounce of dried wild mushrooms in 1 cup of boiling water for 15 minutes. Using a fork, remove the mushrooms from the liquid, and chop finely. Add to 1 pound of domesticated mushrooms for a boost of flavor, then strain the soaking liquid and use it to deglaze the pan with the white wine.

Cornmeal–Cream Cheese Pastry

Makes six 6-inch hand-piecrusts,
or two 12-inch piecrusts

Use for hand pies or for any recipe where you want a soft, flaky pastry with a bit of crunch.

2 cups all-purpose flour

½ cup yellow cornmeal

1 tablespoon granulated sugar

2 teaspoons fresh thyme leaves

1 teaspoon kosher salt

½ cup butter, cut into ½-inch cubes, at room temperature

¼ cup cream cheese, cut into ½-inch cubes, at room temperature

¼ cup ice water

1 egg yolk

1 teaspoon white vinegar or fresh lemon juice

In a large bowl, combine the flour, cornmeal, sugar, thyme, and salt and stir together. Add the butter and cream cheese, working them into the flour with your fingertips until they are pea-size lumps. Make a well in the bottom of the bowl.

In a liquid measuring cup, whisk together the ice water, egg yolk, and vinegar. Pour the liquid into the well, then use your fingertips to bring the dough together into large clumps.

Pour the dough and any loose flour from the bowl onto a work surface; knead quickly and lightly into a ball. Divide the dough in half and form into two 1-inch-thick discs. Wrap tightly in plastic wrap and refrigerate for at least 1 hour, or up to 1 day.

Let the pastry rest on the counter for 5 to 15 minutes to warm slightly before using.

Variation

To make the pastry in a food processor, add the flour, cornmeal, sugar, thyme, and salt to the bowl. Pulse three times to combine. Scatter the butter and cream cheese onto the flour, then pulse five or six times, until you have mostly pea-size lumps. Whisk together the ice water, egg yolk, and vinegar. Add to the bowl and pulse another five times. Pour the dough and any loose flour onto a work surface and proceed as directed.

"Would you like to come back to my house for a little late lunch?
I make a pretty mean stir-fry for an old gal who can't keep track
of her earrings."

"I'd love to. I'll tell you what I know, but it's going to take
awhile. When I talked to Bill this morning, I gave him the *Reader's
Digest* version."

INSOMNIA

Lois's Spicy Stir-Fry

Makes 4 servings

Lack of sleep, bald doctors from another dimension, not to mention an airborne battle with the Crimson King—Ralph and Lois Roberts's love story is a bit on the wild side; you might even say a little spicy.

Don't be scared by the long inventory of ingredients; once the tofu is under the press, you've got time to collect and prepare the rest of the list or even start a pot of rice to go on the side. When that's done, the recipe comes together quickly. If cooking for vegans, substitute an equal amount of brown sugar for the honey.

1 pound extra-firm tofu, drained

3½ tablespoons soy sauce

2 tablespoons honey

2 tablespoons dry sherry

2 tablespoons water

1 tablespoon chili garlic sauce or sriracha

2 garlic cloves, finely grated or minced

½-inch piece ginger, peeled and finely grated

1 teaspoon cornstarch, plus 4 tablespoons

4 tablespoons refined coconut oil or vegetable oil

1 small yellow onion, cut into ½-inch-thick julienne

4 celery stalks, halved lengthwise, cut crosswise into ½-inch pieces

8 button mushrooms, quartered

1 red bell pepper, cut into ½-inch strips

1 pound asparagus, woody ends removed, cut into 1-inch pieces, tips kept separate

½ cup unsalted roasted cashews

2 green onions, white and green parts, chopped

Place a clean, folded dish towel on a dinner plate and set the tofu on top. Place another plate and then a heavy weight, such as a cast-iron pan or heavy book, on top of the tofu to press out the water. Set aside for 15 minutes.

CONTINUED

Vegetarian

In a small bowl, whisk together 3 tablespoons of the soy sauce, the honey, sherry, water, chili garlic sauce, garlic, ginger, and 1 teaspoon cornstarch. Set this sauce aside.

Remove the tofu from under the weight, cut into 1-inch cubes, and toss in a medium bowl with the remaining ½ tablespoon soy sauce. Sprinkle 2 tablespoons cornstarch over the tofu and toss again. Add the remaining 2 tablespoons cornstarch to ensure every tofu piece is evenly coated.

In a large skillet or wok over medium-high heat, melt 2 tablespoons of the coconut oil until shimmering. Add the tofu, in batches if necessary to avoid crowding the pan, and fry, turning occasionally, until golden and crisp on all sides, 5 to 7 minutes per batch. Transfer to a plate and tent lightly with aluminum foil to keep warm.

Add the remaining 2 tablespoons coconut oil to the skillet and let melt. Then the yellow onion, celery, mushrooms, bell pepper, and asparagus (except the tips) and fry, stirring frequently, until the vegetables are crisp-tender, 4 to 5 minutes. Add the asparagus tips and cashews and cook for 2 minutes more. Stir the sauce to recombine and pour over the vegetables in the pan, tossing to coat until the sauce has thickened, about 30 seconds.

Pour the vegetables onto a serving platter, top with the crispy tofu, garnish with the green onions, and serve immediately.

Note

Almost any vegetable works in a stir-fry. If you prefer carrots to bell peppers, or shiitakes to button mushrooms, or the green beans look better than the out-of-season asparagus, use those instead! Adjust the cooking times accordingly and remember to include a variety of colors and shapes. We eat with our eyes first, after all.

They ate a tasty vegetarian casserole (Missy), au gratin potatoes with a cheesy sauce (Myra), and topped the meal off with a lumpy but tasty angel food cake that was only slightly burned on the bottom (Doctor Bob). The wine was good, but the talk and the laughter were better.

When they were finished, he said: "Time to fess up. I've been lying to you. This has been going quite a bit faster than I said it was."

ELEVATION

Missy's Stovetop Millet Casserole with Peanut Sauce

Makes 4 servings

This recipe offers a simple and homely, yet delicious, millet casserole that is full of vegetables and delivers a big flavor punch thanks to the peanut sauce drizzle. Leftovers keep well in an airtight container in the fridge for up to 3 days.

Missy Donaldson wouldn't like to hear it, I'm sure, but this makes a tasty side when served with Pioneer Drumsticks (page 77).

PEANUT SAUCE

½ cup creamy peanut butter

½ cup light coconut milk

1½ tablespoons fresh lime juice, or as needed

2 teaspoons soy sauce, or as needed

1½ teaspoons granulated sugar

CASSEROLE

2 medium celery stalks, roughly chopped

1 medium carrot, peeled and grated

1 medium yellow onion, roughly chopped

¼ cup olive oil

1 small yellow zucchini, grated

2 garlic cloves, grated or minced

1-inch piece ginger, peeled and grated or minced

2 teaspoons ground cumin

1½ teaspoons ground coriander

1 teaspoon kosher salt

½ teaspoon freshly ground black pepper

¼ teaspoon cayenne pepper

1 tablespoon tomato paste

¾ cup uncooked millet

1 cup light coconut milk

¾ cup water

¼ cup unsalted roasted peanuts

Fresh cilantro or parsley for garnishing

CONTINUED

To make the peanut sauce: In the bowl of a small food processor, combine the peanut butter, coconut milk, lime juice, soy sauce, and sugar and process until smooth, 20 to 30 seconds. Taste and adjust the lime juice and soy sauce, if desired. Pour into a bowl, cover, and set aside. Rinse and dry the bowl of the food processor.

To make the casserole: In the bowl of the small food processor, combine the celery, carrot, and onion and pulse until finely chopped.

In a Dutch oven or large saucepan over medium-high heat, warm the olive oil until shimmering. Add the chopped vegetables and zucchini and cook, stirring occasionally, until the vegetables have released their liquid and are starting to turn golden, about 10 minutes. Add the garlic and ginger and stir until fragrant, about 30 seconds.

Add the cumin, coriander, salt, black pepper, and cayenne to the vegetables. Then add the tomato paste and stir continuously for 1 minute. Stir in the millet and then pour in the coconut milk and water. Bring to a boil, turn the heat to low, cover, and cook until the millet is tender, 45 to 50 minutes. Remove from the heat and stir in the peanuts.

Spoon the casserole into bowls, garnish with cilantro, and serve, passing the peanut sauce at the table.

They ate, and they ate well. The food was meatless but terrific:
enchiladas with frijoles and tortillas that had obviously not come
from a supermarket package. As they ate, Scott told Ellis about his
little set-to in Patsy's and about the posters featuring Deirdre
McComb, soon to be replaced by less controversial ones starring a
flock of cartoon turkeys. He asked if Myra had been on that committee.

"No, that's one she missed . . . but I'm sure she would have approved
the change."

ELEVATION

Holy Frijole Enchiladas

Makes 4 servings

Topped with crema, these enchiladas—homemade refried beans rolled in soft corn tortillas and baked in a mild sauce made from roasted California and ancho chiles—make a memorable, special-occasion meal when served with Green Plantain Chips with Mojo Sauce (page 161) for the whole Holy Frijole experience.

This is a big recipe that takes some time, so I usually double it, freezing one batch of twelve enchiladas, with sauce, in a 9 by 13-inch baking dish. To serve, remove from the freezer and bake from frozen, adding a few minutes to the cooking time if necessary.

REFRIED BEANS

1 cup dried pinto beans

1 medium white onion, quartered

1 jalapeño chile, halved lengthwise, stemmed, and seeded

1 garlic clove, peeled

Kosher salt

3 tablespoons refined coconut oil

ENCHILADA SAUCE

6 California chiles (see Notes)

2 ancho chiles (see Notes)

2 cups boiling water

2 tablespoons vegetable oil

2 garlic cloves, crushed

2 teaspoons ground cumin

1 teaspoon granulated sugar

½ teaspoon kosher salt

Vegetable oil for frying

12 yellow corn tortillas (see page 230)

1½ cups shredded Monterey Jack cheese

1 small white onion, finely chopped

Crema or sour cream for drizzling

Lime wedges for squeezing

CONTINUED

To make the refried beans: In a Dutch oven or other large, heavy pot, combine the beans, three-fourths of the onion, the jalapeño, garlic, and 1 teaspoon salt. Add enough cold water to cover by 3 inches and set over medium-high heat. Bring to a low boil, then turn the heat to low and simmer, cooking the beans until they are very soft, about 2 hours. Drain the beans, discarding the jalapeño and reserving 1 cup of the cooking liquid. Wash and dry the Dutch oven.

Finely chop the remaining one-fourth of the onion. In the Dutch oven over medium heat, melt the coconut oil until shimmering. Add the chopped onion and drained beans. Cook until the mixture begins to bubble and spit, 5 to 8 minutes. Ladle in the bean-cooking liquid, about 1/3 cup at a time, while gently stirring and smashing the beans with the back of a large spoon. After all the liquid has been added, continue cooking until the beans are thick and creamy with a few nearly whole beans for texture, lowering the heat as needed to prevent scorching, 10 to 15 minutes. Taste and season with salt. Transfer to a bowl, let cool, and refrigerate until needed, up to 5 days. Wash and dry the Dutch oven.

To make the enchilada sauce: Position an oven rack on the middle rung, set the Dutch oven on it, and heat the oven to 350°F.

Add all the chiles to the hot pan in the oven and roast, stirring once, until aromatic and lightly browned, up to 5 minutes. Do not let them burn. Turn off the oven.

In a medium bowl, combine the chiles and boiling water. Let soak, turning the chiles occasionally, until they are soft and dark red, 20 to 30 minutes. Drain the chiles, reserving the soaking water. Discard the stems, slice the chiles open lengthwise, and briefly dip each into the reserved soaking water to wash off the seeds. Add the chiles to the bowl of a blender or food processor. Strain and reserve the soaking water, discarding the seeds.

In a large skillet over medium heat, warm the 2 tablespoons vegetable oil until shimmering. Add the garlic and cook until light golden, stirring occasionally, about 2 minutes. Add the garlic to the chiles, reserving the oil in the pan. Process the chiles and garlic with enough of the reserved soaking water to make a puree the thickness of whipping cream. Add the cumin, sugar, and salt and puree until smooth, about 1 minute. Pour the sauce into the reserved oil in the pan and warm over medium heat until simmering; turn the heat to low to keep warm.

Heat the oven to 400°F. Line a baking sheet with parchment paper and lightly brush or spray with vegetable oil.

In a medium skillet over medium-high heat, warm ½ inch of vegetable oil until shimmering and almost smoking. Using tongs, lay a tortilla in the oil and cook until slightly crisp, 10 to 15 seconds. Over the skillet, shake off the excess oil from the tortilla, dip the tortilla in the enchilada sauce to coat, and transfer to a plate. Spread a heaping spoonful of beans across the center of the tortilla, then sprinkle sparingly with the cheese and finely chopped onion, reserving a fourth of the cheese for the top. Roll and arrange on the prepared baking sheet; repeat with the remaining tortillas, sauce, beans, cheese, and onion.

Drizzle the enchiladas with the rest of the sauce, top with the reserved cheese, and bake until they have softened and sunk, 30 to 35 minutes. Let cool on a wire rack for 5 minutes.

Divide the enchiladas three to a plate, drizzle with the crema, and serve immediately, passing the lime wedges for squeezing at the table.

Notes

The mix of California and ancho chiles results in a mild, flavorful sauce suitable for all ages and palates. For more heat, use an equal amount of New Mexico chiles instead of California. Substituting guajillo chiles for the anchos will increase the heat further and lend a delicious smoky-fruitiness to the sauce.

Dried chiles, even the mild varieties, vary in heat. Because the pith and seeds contain most of the burn, wear gloves when handling, and wash your hands when you're done.

Burned chiles produce a bitter, unpalatable sauce. If you burn them, discard and begin again.

Side Dishes

The kitchen wasn't the only place I learned from my mama. She had the greenest of thumbs, especially in the vegetable garden. From greens and garlic to potatoes and zucchini, she grew it all. Nothing grows as well in my garden as in hers, except maybe my green beans. The string beans of her garden are gone, replaced by my tender and slender stringless ones. She was also the one who taught me to forage in the woods. In the spring, we looked for nettles, fiddleheads, and hard-to-find ramps. In the fall, it was for mushrooms—skills I passed on to my Ray—we may not have always had meat on the table, but we never starved. There's a lot of food in the wilds of Maine, if you know where to look.

Never venture out without that knowing. Most fools know mushrooms can be deadly, but even some Mainers, mostly city folk like Trisha McFarland from down in Sanford, have no idea that eating fiddleheads raw, straight from the fern, will give you a bad case of food poisoning. Oooh, that poor girl must have had some terrible cramps!

Between the forests and the sea, Maine is fertile land, including the fields of potatoes that grow up on the Canadian border in Aroostook. I always make a full recipe of potato stuffing, even when it was just Ray and me, so that I have leftovers for a blue plate special. My mouth waters just thinking of that gravy on that stuffing.

No one believes me when I tell them you can make french fries at home without a lot of mess, but I prove them wrong every time. I blanch potato sticks in water, sugar, and salt for flavor before covering them with cold oil. The fries poach in the oil while it warms, before it gets hot enough to crisp up the outsides.

And while I doubt Dolores Claiborne ever heard of risotto out on Big Tall Island, I can see her in my mind's eye, a soft young bride with the rice still in her hair, and I know from my own experience how she hardened over the years of struggle and survival. It's in her honor that I've created a one-pot, oven-baked risotto that makes it easy to put comfort on the table.

Comfort can come from the most unlikely of places when you're desperate, including from the vegetables you despised as a kid. Enjoy these side dishes (mostly) from my youth.

Those dark green ferns weren't just ferns, (Trisha) thought; she had been fiddleheading with her mother and grandmother three springs in a row, and she thought those were fiddleheads. Fiddleheads were over in Sanford—had been for at least a month—but her mother had told her they came into season quite a bit later inland, almost up until July in especially marshy places. . . .

THE GIRL WHO LOVED TOM GORDON

There was a gravel area on the far side of the Extension, outside the
Cyclone fence marking the county airport's property. Lots of people
set up roadside stands there during the busy hours of the day, because
it was possible for customers to pull in without getting tailgated
(if you were quick and remembered to use your blinker, that was).
Streeter had lived his whole life in the little Maine city of Derry,
and over the years he'd seen people selling fresh fiddleheads there
in the spring, fresh berries and corn on the cob in the summer, and
lobsters almost year-round. . . .

"FAIR EXTENSION"

Roadside Fiddleheads

Makes 4 servings

Fiddleheads are the new shoots from an ostrich fern, native here in the Northeast. Their season lasts just two weeks in April or May, but it's worth searching them out for their deliciously green, earthy flavor. Once thoroughly washed, they must be steamed or blanched for 10 minutes to eliminate the chance of foodborne illness.

Pick them yourself, or pull up to a local roadside stand for a bag or two. Fresh is best, but sometimes I'll ask a neighbor for a jar of preserved fiddleheads so I can make this out of season.

If you're ever in Derry, be sure to avoid a man by the name of George Edvil, sitting behind his card table on the far side of the Harris Avenue Extension. The sign may say fair price, but his deals are rarely what they seem.

3 cups fiddlehead ferns, cleaned of their papery skins
3 tablespoons butter
1 garlic clove, finely grated or minced
2 teaspoons fresh lemon juice
Kosher salt
Freshly ground black pepper

In a large bowl, rinse the fiddleheads, changing the water three or four times, to ensure the papery skin and grit are all gone.

In a large saucepan fitted with a vegetable steamer, bring ½ inch of water to a boil. Add the fiddleheads and steam, covered, until crisp-tender, at least 10 minutes or up to 12 minutes.

In a large skillet over medium-high heat, melt the butter until bubbling. Add the garlic and stir until fragrant, about 45 seconds. Add the fiddleheads and cook, tossing constantly, until warmed through and well coated with the garlic butter, 2 to 5 minutes more. Add the lemon juice and toss one last time. Taste and season with salt and pepper.

Serve the fiddleheads immediately.

"Most of the people he's meeting with think that if Reagan is nominated over Ford next year, it's going to mean the death of the party," Sarah said. "And if the Grand Old Party dies, that means Walt won't be able to run for Bill Cohen's seat in 1978 when Cohen goes after Bill Hathaway's Senate seat."

Herb was watching Denny eat string beans, seriously, one by one, using all six of his teeth on them. "I don't think Cohen will be able to wait until '78 to get in the Senate. He'll run against Muskie next year."

THE DEAD ZONE

Grand Ol' String Beans

Makes 4 servings

This simple side features fresh snap beans, straight from the pole or bush, given a flavor boost with an old Yankee favorite, salt pork.

These days it seems everyone cooks their beans for just 2 or 3 minutes, but I prefer to blanch them a few minutes longer, which brings out the most flavor but stops short of turning them to olive-green mush.

1½ teaspoons kosher salt
1 pound green beans
2-inch cube salt pork, diced
2 small shallots, julienned
¼ teaspoon freshly ground black pepper

In a large pot over high heat, bring 3 inches of water and 1 teaspoon of the salt to a boil. Line a small plate with a double layer of paper towels.

Trim and discard the ends of the green beans. Add the green beans to the boiling water and blanch until tender, 5 to 6 minutes. Drain and toss the beans to allow the steam to escape so that they dry.

Put the salt pork in a large, cold cast-iron skillet or other heavy pan. Set over medium heat and render the fat from the pork, stirring occasionally, until crisp, 8 to 10 minutes. Using a slotted spoon, transfer the pork to the prepared plate.

Add the shallots to the skillet and sweat until soft and translucent, about 5 minutes. Add the green beans, season with the remaining ½ teaspoon salt and the pepper, and sauté until warm, about 3 minutes more.

Transfer the green beans to a serving platter, garnish with the crisp salt pork, and serve immediately.

"We have lots of broccoli when Aunt Hilda comes. None of us like it, and it just about makes my sister puke, but Aunt Hilda likes broccoli a lot, so we have it. There was a book on our summer reading list, *Great Expectations*, and there was a lady in it who was just like Aunt Hilda. She got her kicks dangling her money in front of her relatives. Her name was Miss Havisham, and when Miss Havisham said frog, people jumped. We jump, and I guess the rest of our family does, too."

"THE SUN DOG"

Blue Cheese Broccoli

Makes 4 servings

This is an easy weeknight side dish using the favorite vegetable of Kevin Delevan's not-so-favorite aunt. Also from what I hear, he was quite the young photographer. It's a great way to use up leftover salad dressing; I prefer it with my French dressing, but almost any vinaigrette will do.

1 pound broccoli crowns
½ cup Nouveau French Dressing (page 230) or other vinaigrette
1 tablespoon olive oil
½ teaspoon kosher salt
¼ teaspoon freshly ground black pepper
⅓ cup crumbled blue cheese

Position an oven rack on the bottom rung and heat the oven to 425°F. Line a baking sheet with parchment paper.

Divide the broccoli into florets about 2 inches wide, each with a substantial stalk. Make the pieces all roughly the same size so that they cook in the same amount of time. In a large bowl, toss the broccoli with the dressing, olive oil, salt, and pepper.

Arrange the broccoli in a single layer on the prepared baking sheet and bake until golden on the bottom, 10 to 12 minutes. Flip the broccoli, scatter the blue cheese over the top, and return it to the oven until the cheese is melted and the broccoli is browned on the other side, 8 to 10 minutes more. The more crispy, golden brown bits, the more flavor.

Transfer the broccoli to a plate and serve immediately.

When [Missy] returned, she brought appetizers with their drinks, setting the plates down almost reverently. The smell was to die for.

"What have we got here?" Scott asked.

"Freshly fried green plantain chips, and a salsa of garlic, cilantro, lime, and a little green chile. Compliments of the chef. She says it's more Cuban than Mexican, but she hopes that won't keep you from enjoying it."

———

ELEVATION

Green Plantain Chips with Mojo Sauce

Makes 6 servings

This is Missy Donaldson's recipe for tostones—twice-fried Cuban-style green plantains—served with mojo sauce on the side.

Holy frijole, indeed. That woman could cook! Once she and her wife, Deirdre, broke through the town's Yankee defenses and showed Castle Rock what it had been missing, their restaurant was always full. There's nothing like good food to attract new friends.

Vegetable oil for frying
2 large green plantains
Table salt or fine sea salt
Mojo Sauce (recipe follows) for serving

Line a plate with a double layer of paper towels. In a Dutch oven or deep skillet over high heat, warm 1½ inches of vegetable oil to 350°F. Keep watch on the oil as you proceed to peel the plantains.

Using a sharp knife, trim both ends off the plantains. Then, using the tip of the knife, score the skin of each plantain lengthwise, from top to bottom, in three places, trying not to cut into the flesh. Working from one end, peel and discard the strips of skins. Slice the plantains into 2-inch-thick rounds.

Add the plantain slices to the oil, in batches if necessary to avoid overcrowding the pan, and fry, turning occasionally, until softened, about 5 minutes. Using a slotted spoon, transfer to the prepared plate to drain. Temporarily remove the oil from the heat.

CONTINUED

Place a plantain on a cutting board and cover with a paper towel folded in half. Press down on the plantain with your palm to smash it into a disc ¼ to ½ inch thick. Repeat with the remaining plantains.

Line the plate with a new double layer of paper towels.

Reheat the oil to 350°F, add the smashed plantains, and fry, turning occasionally, until golden brown and crisp, 4 to 5 minutes. Transfer to the prepared plate to drain, then taste and season with salt.

Place the plantains on a clean plate and serve immediately with the mojo sauce for dipping.

Mojo Sauce

Makes about 1 cup

Serve with tostones or use it as a marinade and dip for oven-roasted chicken wings.

1 cup firmly packed fresh cilantro
¼ cup olive oil
¼ cup fresh orange juice
3 tablespoons fresh lime juice
1 serrano chile, stemmed and chopped (see Note)
1 garlic clove, quartered
1 teaspoon granulated sugar
½ teaspoon kosher salt

In the bowl of a small food processor, combine the cilantro, olive oil, orange juice, lime juice, chile, garlic, sugar, and salt and blend until smooth, about 45 seconds.

Transfer the sauce to a small bowl to serve.

Note
Too spicy? Remove the seeds and pith from the chile.

"Sit down," he said. "We've got a five-course lunch, courtesy of Castle Rock Variety—grinders, which are for some strange reason called 'Italian sandwiches' up here . . . mozzarella sticks . . . garlic fries . . . Twinkies."

"That's only four," I said.

BAG OF BONES

Garlic Fries

Makes 4 servings

We always used Kennebec potatoes, named after Maine's great river, for our fries, but russets work just fine in a pinch. If you're in a hurry, or don't like the takeout taste that the sugar-salt brine lends the fries, you can skip the blanching step and start the raw potatoes directly in the cold oil; they'll take an extra 3 or 4 minutes to cook crisp.

Serve with or without the garlic sauce as a component of Moose-Lickit Fish and Chips (page 117) for a homemade fish fry straight from the fish shack I worked at my first summer after finishing high school.

¼ cup olive oil

¼ cup chopped fresh parsley

2 tablespoons grated Parmesan cheese

2 garlic cloves, chopped

4 teaspoons kosher salt

2 pounds white potatoes (such as Kennebec or russet)

½ cup granulated sugar

1½ to 2 quarts vegetable oil

In the bowl of a small food processor, combine the olive oil, parsley, Parmesan, garlic, and 1 teaspoon of the salt and process until well combined, about 30 seconds. Set this sauce aside.

In a Dutch oven or other large, heavy pot, bring 2 quarts of water to a boil. Peel the potatoes and cut them lengthwise into ¼- to ⅜-inch-thick slices. Stack the slices and cut them into sticks ¼ to ⅜ inch thick.

Stir the sugar and remaining 3 teaspoons salt into the boiling water. Add the potatoes, cover, remove from the heat, and let blanch for 15 minutes. Drain, then spread the potatoes in a single layer on a baking sheet and set aside for 5 to 10 minutes to dry out.

CONTINUED

Line a large bowl with a double layer of paper towels. Rinse and dry the Dutch oven.

Transfer the potatoes into the Dutch oven and add enough of the vegetable oil to just cover. Set over high heat and cook, stirring once at 2 minutes and again at 7 minutes. The fries become a bit fragile at this stage, so allow them to cook untouched until they begin to crisp, 12 to 15 minutes. Continue to cook, stirring occasionally, until they are crisp on the outside and tender on the inside, 18 to 22 minutes more, depending on the thickness of the fries.

Using a slotted spoon, transfer the fries to the prepared bowl to drain. Then remove the paper towels from the bowl, spoon in the garlic sauce, and toss well until all the fries are coated.

Divide the garlic fries onto plates and serve immediately.

Notes

Cut a thin slice from the bottom of each potato before you slice it lengthwise; the potato will sit flat on the cutting board, making it easier and safer to slice.

When the oil has cooled, strain it and refrigerate in a covered container. Reuse the fry oil four or five times before using it one last time for Lobster Pickin's (page 95), fried clams (see page 107), or a batch of chicken wings. Discard it after that.

Potato Stuffing

Makes 8 servings

From Nate Hoppenstand's family up in Aroostook, Maine's potato country, to generations of Pennsylvania Dutch—as well as Canadians up the Yale Line in New Brunswick—everyone claims this stuffing as their own. It's a surprisingly light combination of two favorite sides that leaves room for more vegetables on the table.

My family's mixture of leeks, mushrooms, and water chestnuts is unusual, but I've never seen anyone pass up seconds. We always baked it in its own dish, topped with bacon for extra flavor, but you can stuff your holiday turkey with it too.

6 slices bread, cut into ½-inch cubes

Kosher salt

2 pounds russet potatoes, peeled and chopped into 2-inch pieces

½ cup butter

2 cups chopped leeks, white and light green parts only

1 cup chopped celery

1 cup chopped mushrooms

Freshly ground black pepper

1 tablespoon Bell's Seasoning, or other poultry seasoning (see Note)

One 8-ounce can sliced water chestnuts, drained

2 eggs, lightly beaten

4 slices bacon (optional)

Position an oven rack on the upper-middle rung and heat the broiler. Spread the bread cubes on a baking sheet and toast under the broiler until just lightly golden, 3 to 5 minutes. Set aside.

Turn off the broiler and heat the oven to 350°F. Butter a 9 by 13-inch baking dish.

In a large pot over medium-high heat, combine 1 inch of water, ½ teaspoon salt, and the potatoes. Cover and bring to a boil, then turn the heat to medium-low and simmer until tender, about 15 minutes. Drain and gently toss the potatoes around to dry them. Cover to keep warm.

In a large, heavy pan over medium heat, melt the butter until bubbling. Add the leeks, celery, and mushrooms; taste and season with salt and pepper; and sauté, stirring constantly, until softened and translucent, about 10 minutes. Add the Bell's and continue to cook until fragrant, about 1 minute more.

Add the sautéed vegetables, toasted bread cubes, water chestnuts, and eggs to the pot with the potatoes, gently stirring to break up the potatoes but leaving some chunks for texture. Taste and season with salt and pepper.

Spoon the stuffing into the prepared baking dish and lay the bacon (if using) across the top. Bake until the top is golden and the bacon is starting to crisp, about 45 minutes. Remove from the oven and let cool for 10 minutes.

Serve the stuffing hot.

Note
If you prefer to use fresh herbs, use 2 tablespoons minced sage, 1 tablespoon minced rosemary, and 1 tablespoon minced thyme instead of the poultry seasoning.

Mrs. Turman brought Billy and me each a plate, garnished with helpings of deli potato salad. I ate as best I could, but Billy would not even pick at his.

"You got to eat, big guy," I said.

"I'm not hungry," he said, putting the plate aside.

"You can't get big and strong if you don't—"

Mrs. Turman, sitting slightly behind Billy, shook her head at me.

"Okay," I said. "Go get a peach and eat it, at least. 'Kay?"

—————

"THE MIST"

Deli Potato Salad

Makes 6 servings

The first of the thinnies, those weak spots in reality, that I ever heard about was the thick mist that appeared over Bridgton, near Federal Foods. I've never been trapped inside a grocery store, but I can imagine worse places to be than surrounded by food. I'd eat the refrigerated stuff first, before the generators run out.

Here's my favorite recipe for deli-style potato salad, adapted to perfection over a lifetime. If you have leftovers, store them in the fridge for up to 3 days.

½ cup mayonnaise

2 tablespoons olive oil

1 tablespoon Dijon mustard

1 tablespoon gherkin juice, plus 2 tablespoons finely diced gherkins

1½ teaspoons kosher salt

½ teaspoon freshly ground black pepper

¼ teaspoon cayenne pepper

½ cup shredded carrot

½ cup finely diced celery

¼ cup minced green onions, white and green parts

2 pounds red potatoes, scrubbed clean

In a large bowl, whisk together the mayonnaise, olive oil, mustard, gherkin juice, 1 teaspoon of the salt, black pepper, and cayenne. Stir in the carrot, celery, green onions, and diced gherkins; set aside.

Cut the potatoes into quarters lengthwise, then crosswise into ½-inch-thick slices. In a large pot, combine 1 inch of cold water and the remaining ½ teaspoon salt. Add the potatoes, cover, and set over medium-high heat. Boil, then lower the heat to a simmer and cook until fork-tender, 6 to 8 minutes.

Drain and gently toss the potatoes around to dry them. Add to the dressing and toss to combine. Serve the potato salad warm or chilled.

Dolores's Oven Risotto

Makes 6 servings

That wastrel husband of Dolores Claiborne deserved what he got, despite what some out on Little Tall Island think and say. Dolores worked her hands to the bone keeping house for that drunk pervert, and sometimes, as Vera Donovan was fond of saying, "an accident can be an unhappy woman's best friend."

Serve this risotto with Mother Morton's Pork Chops (page 73) and Blue Cheese Broccoli (page 159) for a simple, comforting meal that will chase your troubles away.

3 cups chicken stock (see page 233) or vegetable stock

½ ounce dried wild mushrooms (such as porcini or chanterelle)

¾ cup boiling water

2 tablespoons olive oil

3 garlic cloves, finely grated or minced

1 cup carnaroli or arborio rice

⅔ cup grated Parmesan cheese, plus more for serving

1 tablespoon butter

2 teaspoons fresh lemon juice

Kosher salt

Position an oven rack on the lower-middle rung and heat the oven to 400°F.

In a medium pot over medium heat, warm the chicken stock to a simmer. Soak the mushrooms in the boiling water for 15 minutes. Using a fork, scoop the mushrooms from the liquid and chop finely. Strain the soaking liquid and add it to the stock.

CONTINUED

In a Dutch oven or other large, ovenproof pot over medium heat, warm the olive oil until shimmering. Add the garlic and rice and cook, stirring constantly, until the grains of rice are transparent, about 2 minutes. Stir in the mushrooms and stock and bring to a boil.

Cover the Dutch oven, transfer to the oven, and bake until the rice is al dente, about 20 minutes. Stir in the Parmesan, butter, and lemon juice and then taste and season with salt.

Serve the risotto hot, passing additional Parmesan at the table.

Baking and Sweets

Ask any cook and they'll tell you; it's the baking and sweets that people remember. You can cook a five-course meal with all the fixings, and they'll eat their fill of those first four courses, raving the whole time. But when the dessert comes out at the last, appetite and memory reset themselves, and the sweets always take the cake.

Even when the times demanded I be a workhorse in the kitchen and the garden to keep us fed, baking was always my respite. The baby-bottom feel of silky dough under my kneading hands, the smell of it as it turns to bread in the oven, the sound of doughnuts bubbling and crisping in shortening, the sharp sweet bite of a stolen spoonful of lemon curd, and the magic velvet of a custard as it thickens before my eyes; I love every sensual minute of it. I'm not one to wax flowery about this kind of thing, but my baking time is near sacred to me.

If I remember right, my farmhouse loaf recipe originally came from a big-city paper, likely Boston or New York. Over the years, the recipe changed from a traditional challah; I use butter rather than oil now, and instead of braiding it, I bake it in loaf pans for sandwiches. It keeps beautifully, and is the best bread for French toast and stuffing.

Boston brown bread, as it's known outside New England, is a quick bread with or without raisins, leavened with baking powder and soda, and served at bean suppers across the region. It was traditionally steamed in coffee cans on the stove top, but big cans of coffee are hard to come by these days, so I bake it in a loaf pan in the oven, using a water bath for steam to soften the cornmeal.

My muffin, hermit, and shortcake recipes all use Bakewell Cream. A response to a shortage of cream of tartar during WWII, we've relied on it ever since to give an extra-light rise to our biscuits and baked goods. Try it if you can find it, and see what you think. If you can't get a hold of it, there are instructions for substituting with baking powder in the recipe Notes, as well as on page 6 (see "Bakewell Cream").

Rich, sweet, and crumbly, the fig bars are based on a recipe for date squares that my mother-in-law gave to me on my wedding day, to keep her precious boy happy. I did what I did with pretty much everything I got from that woman, including her son—I made some changes—figs replace the dates, and my bars are flavored with orange and cardamom.

My favorite dessert recipe here is one I created over the years in honor of Maine's official dessert, blueberry pie, and the Creator's favorite brain food, New York–style cheesecake. Fresh glazed berries sit atop a rich, yet light-tasting cheesecake, all nestled in a buttery homemade crust.

Another very special recipe is the family recipe for strawberry shortcake. My mom's mom made this once a year, every June, for Grandpa's birthday. When it came time to clean up, Grandma always shared the small shortcake she had cut from the middle of the biscuit, layered with more strawberries and cream, with her helpers in the kitchen. By then, the strawberry juice had soaked all the way through the biscuit and the cream had become a bit stiff. It was a crumbly, sweet, juicy mess—you've never seen so many kids clamoring to clear the table!

Any other time she served strawberry shortcake, she'd pat the dough out and use a biscuit cutter to cut out individual biscuits, then bake them as directed in Sausage on Cheese Biscuits to Go (page 27). She'd split them and dress them just the same as the big one.

See what I'm saying? It's the sweets and baking we remember.

They came up onto the platform one by one and stood behind a long trestle table covered with a linen cloth. The table was stacked high with pies and stood at the edge of the platform. Above it were looped necklaces of bare 100-watt bulbs, moths and night-fliers banging softly against them and haloing them. Above the platform, bathed in spotlights, was a long sign which read: The Great Gretna Pie-Eat of 1960! . . .

"THE BODY"

Farmhouse Egg Bread

Makes two 1½-pound loaves

I believe that the devil passed through Motton that day, and I believe he scared the bejesus out of poor Gary. No boy or man would claim to have been saved by a fish unless it was true, and stranger things have happened in that corner of Maine.

This egg bread begins as a soft, sticky enriched dough and transforms into a fine-crumbed, long-keeping loaf that is perfect for toast and sandwiches. Cut slices from a still-warm loaf to make your own jelly fold-overs, and use the second loaf to make Dog Days French Toast Casserole (page 17).

3 eggs

1 teaspoon cold (50°F) water,
plus 2 cups warm (105°F) water

6 cups all-purpose flour

3 tablespoons granulated sugar

4½ teaspoons instant yeast

1 tablespoon kosher salt

¼ cup butter, cut into small pieces,
at room-temperature

1 teaspoon vegetable oil

Sesame seeds or poppy seeds
for garnishing (optional)

In a medium bowl, whisk the eggs until well combined. In a small bowl, combine 1 tablespoon of the beaten egg with the cold water to make an egg wash. Cover and refrigerate.

In the bowl of a stand mixer fitted with the paddle attachment, combine the flour, sugar, yeast, and salt. Mix on low speed. While the machine is running, scatter in the pieces of butter. Pour in the warm water and beaten eggs and turn the speed to medium-low, mixing to form a rough ball. Switch to the bread hook, scrape down the bowl, and knead the mixture on medium-low speed for 5 to 6 minutes, scraping down the bowl once or twice, as needed. The dough should be smooth, elastic, and a little sticky.

CONTINUED

Pour the vegetable oil over the dough and, using a dough scraper, toss it to coat. Cover the bowl with a clean dish towel and then a plate. Set the bowl in a warm, draft-free place to rise until the dough is doubled in size, about 1 hour.

Position an oven rack on the lower-middle rung and heat the oven to 375°F. Generously butter two 5 by 9-inch loaf pans.

Transfer the risen dough to a lightly floured work surface and knead several times to de-gas it completely. Divide the dough into two equal pieces and press each piece into a rectangle measuring 5 by 8 inches. Starting on the shorter ends, roll up the dough, using your thumbs to pinch the seam closed after each roll. Pinch the final seams closed, then gently rock the loaves on the work surface, seam-side down. Transfer to the prepared pans, ensuring that the loaves touch both ends of the pan for an even rise.

Loosely cover the pans with plastic wrap and let the dough rise until doubled in size and it has crested the tops of the pans, about 45 minutes. Brush the tops of both loaves gently with the egg wash. Garnish with sesame seeds (if using) and bake, turning the pans halfway through, until the tops are dark golden, the loaves sound hollow when tapped on the bottom, and an instant-read thermometer inserted into the center of the loaf registers 190°F, 30 to 40 minutes.

Remove the loaves from the pans immediately and let cool on a wire rack for 1 hour before slicing.

Note

If you prefer to mix and knead the dough by hand, resist the temptation to over-flour the work surface. Sticky doughs can be tricky to knead by hand, but lightly oiling your hands and using a dough scraper to do the lifting and turning of the dough make the process easier without having to resort to more flour, which will result in less-than-tender loaves.

THE TOMMYKNOCKERS

Brown Bread with Raisins

Makes 1 loaf

Ruth McCausland is a Maine legend. When her husband, a state policeman, died at thirty-seven, she mourned for two years before getting herself elected as Haven's constable. Over the years, she got rid of the town's worst deadbeats, and died trying to save it from alien invaders.

In my house, as it was in Ruth's, there is no such thing as brown bread without raisins. Serve it slathered in butter next to Dick Hallorann's Baked Beans (page 127) or Better-than-Canned Mulligatawny (page 41).

⅔ cup whole-wheat flour

⅔ cup all-purpose flour

⅔ cup cornmeal

1½ teaspoons baking soda

1½ teaspoons baking powder

1 teaspoon kosher salt

1⅓ cups milk

¼ cup molasses

2 tablespoons dark brown sugar

½ cup golden raisins

Position an oven rack on the lower-middle rung and heat the oven to 350°F. Bring a kettle of water to boil. Butter a 5 by 9-inch loaf pan.

In a large bowl, combine both flours, the cornmeal, baking soda, baking powder, and salt. Add the milk, molasses, brown sugar, and raisins and stir to form a smooth and lump-free batter.

Pour the batter into the prepared loaf pan and cover tightly with aluminum foil. Set the pan into a larger baking dish, and half-fill that dish with boiling water. Bake until a skewer inserted in the center of the bread comes out clean, 40 to 45 minutes.

Set the pan on a wire rack and let the bread cool for 15 minutes. Run a knife around the edge of the loaf, invert the pan, and place the bread on the wire rack. Let cool for 30 minutes more before slicing.

Serve while slightly warm or at room temperature.

[Vic] had spent the morning writing ads for Decoster Egg Farms.
It was hard going. He had hated eggs since his boyhood, when his
mother grimly forced one down his throat four days a week. The best
he had been able to come up with so far was eggs say love . . .
seamlessly. Not very good. Seamlessly had given him the idea of a
trick photo which would show an egg with a zipper running around
its middle. . . . Ought to ask the Tadder, he thought, as the
waitress brought him coffee and a blueberry muffin. Tad liked eggs.

———
CUJO

Blueberry–Lemon Curd Muffins

Makes 12 muffins

These muffins are a treat and a comfort, combining sweet wild blueberries with tart lemon curd. If you are using frozen berries, ensure they're frozen solid when you add them to the bowl; otherwise, they'll turn the batter blue. The muffins can be stored in an airtight container in the fridge for up to 3 days. Warm gently in a 250°F oven for 5 to 10 minutes to refresh before serving.

1¼ cups granulated sugar,
plus 1 tablespoon

¾ cup buttermilk (see "Buttermilk," page 6)
or milk

¼ cup butter, melted and slightly cooled

¼ cup vegetable oil

2 eggs

2½ cups all-purpose flour

1 tablespoon Bakewell Cream (see Note)

1 teaspoon baking soda

1 teaspoon kosher salt

1½ cups fresh or frozen wild blueberries

½ cup lemon curd (recipe follows)

Position an oven rack on the middle rung and heat the oven to 375°F. Line a 12-cup muffin tin with paper liners.

In a large bowl, whisk together the 1¼ cups sugar, buttermilk, butter, vegetable oil, and eggs. In a medium bowl, whisk together the flour, Bakewell Cream, baking soda, and salt. Gently stir in the blueberries. Add the flour mixture to the wet ingredients and stir until just combined into a batter.

Drop a spoonful of the batter into each muffin cup, top with a heaping 2 teaspoons of the lemon curd and then the rest of the batter, filling each cup to the top. Sprinkle with the remaining 1 tablespoon sugar.

Bake the muffins until golden brown, 20 to 24 minutes. Let cool in the pan for 10 minutes, then transfer to a wire rack and let cool completely before serving.

Note

No Bakewell Cream? Substitute 1 tablespoon baking powder and decrease the baking soda to ¼ teaspoon.

Microwave Lemon Curd

Makes about 2 cups

Use to fill muffins or a tray of lemon squares, or serve with scones and fresh raspberries.

1 cup fresh lemon juice
1 cup granulated sugar
½ cup butter, melted
2 eggs

In a large microwave-safe bowl, whisk together the lemon juice, sugar, butter, and eggs. To avoid boil-overs, ensure the ingredients fill no more than one-fourth of the bowl.

Microwave the mixture on high power in 1-minute increments, stirring to combine after each minute. When the curd starts to thicken and coats the back of a spoon, it is getting close. Watch it carefully; it's ready when it starts to mound as you stir and its temperature registers 185°F on an instant-read thermometer, 4 to 10 minutes, depending on your microwave. Stir the curd one more time.

Strain the mixture through a fine-mesh sieve into a medium metal bowl to catch any bits of cooked egg white. Set on top of a wire rack or trivet, and stir occasionally to cool quickly.

Transfer the curd to an airtight container and store in the refrigerator for up to 1 week.

Ben was neatly stowing his empty wrappers in the lunchbag he had
brought. Both Eddie and Bill had been amazed by the size of the repast
Ben had laid out with businesslike efficiency: two PB&J sandwiches,
one bologna sandwich, a hardcooked egg (complete with a pinch of salt
twisted up in a small piece of waxed paper), two fig-bars, three large
chocolate chip cookies, and a Ring-Ding.

—

IT

Homemade Fig Bars

Makes sixteen 2-inch squares

It's no mystery that Ben Hanscom's weight
was a result of his mother's guilt. I'm not
saying she had anything to feel guilty about;
God knows it's hard enough raising these
kids without their daddies, but she buried
that poor boy in food until he convinced
her he'd rather eat like a rabbit.

One thing for sure, Ben would have had
a hard time turning down one of these
homemade fig bars. Can't wait until they're
cool? Serve a big spoonful straight out of
the oven on a scoop of vanilla ice cream.

8 ounces dried figs, stemmed and chopped

1 cup fresh orange juice, plus grated zest of
1 medium orange

2 tablespoons honey

¼ teaspoon baking soda

1½ cups quick-cooking oats

1 cup whole-wheat flour

¾ cup packed light brown sugar

½ teaspoon ground cardamom

½ teaspoon baking powder

½ teaspoon kosher salt

¾ cup cold butter

Position an oven rack on the middle rung and heat the oven to 350°F. Butter the bottom and sides of an 8-inch square pan. Line the bottom with parchment paper, pressing the sheet into the butter so that it sticks.

In a medium saucepan over medium heat, combine the figs, orange juice, and honey and bring to a boil. Add the baking soda, turn the heat to medium-low, and simmer, stirring occasionally, until the mixture is syrupy and the figs have fallen apart, about 10 minutes. Remove from the heat, stir in the orange zest, and pour onto a plate to cool slightly.

In a large bowl, stir together the oats, flour, brown sugar, cardamom, baking powder, and salt. Grate the butter into the oat mixture and work it with your fingertips until crumbly.

Spread half the oat mixture in the prepared baking dish and press down firmly with slightly damp hands. Spread the fig mixture on top in an even layer. Cover with the remaining oat mixture and press down lightly.

Bake until the top is golden brown, 40 to 45 minutes. Then let cool completely on a wire rack, about 4 hours.

Cut the fig bars into 2-inch squares and store in a covered container at room temperature for up to 5 days.

Garraty took out his cookies, and for a moment turned the foil package over in his hands. He thought homesickly of his mother, then stuffed the feeling aside. He would see Mom and Jan in Freeport. That was a promise. He ate a cookie and felt a little better.

THE LONG WALK

Hermits for the Road

Makes 24 bars

My youngest died at six of pneumonia, the Squads took my husband. Last of all, the Major stole my Ray as a prop for his Walk. I could see Ray wanted me gone from the start line, so I left him there with nothing but a half dozen Hermits wrapped in foil. I scrounged every pantry in the neighborhood for a few of the walnuts he liked so much and folded them into the batter along with the raisins. I like to think they helped.

2½ cups all-purpose flour
1 teaspoon Bakewell Cream (see Note)
1 teaspoon kosher salt
½ teaspoon baking soda
2 teaspoons ground cinnamon
2 teaspoons ground ginger
½ teaspoon freshly grated nutmeg
½ teaspoon ground cloves
½ cup butter, at room temperature
¾ cup packed light brown sugar
2 eggs
⅓ cup molasses
1 cup roughly chopped raisins
¾ cup chopped walnuts
½ cup powdered sugar
1 to 2 tablespoons milk

In a medium bowl, whisk together the flour, Bakewell Cream, salt, baking soda, cinnamon, ginger, nutmeg, and cloves.

In a large bowl, using a handheld mixer on medium speed or a wooden spoon, beat together the butter and brown sugar until thoroughly combined, about 1 minute. Add the eggs and molasses and beat until light and creamy, 1 minute more.

CONTINUED

Add the flour mixture to the creamed mixture in two parts, stirring it in with a wooden spoon until just combined. Fold in the raisins and walnuts, then cover and chill this dough for 30 minutes.

Position an oven rack on the lower-middle rung and heat the oven to 350°F. Line a baking sheet with parchment paper.

Divide the chilled dough into three equal pieces. Roll each piece into a ball and then into a log about 10 inches long. Arrange on the prepared baking sheet, leaving 3 inches between the logs, and flatten the tops with your fingertips.

Bake until the edges are crisp, but not browned, 20 to 30 minutes. Transfer the baking sheet to a wire rack to let cool.

In a small bowl, stir together the powdered sugar and enough of the milk until this icing is smooth but not too runny.

When the logs are still slightly warm, drizzle the icing over them and allow it to harden.

Cut the hermits on the diagonal into 1-inch-wide bars and store in an airtight container at room temperature for up to 2 weeks.

Note

No Bakewell Cream? Substitute 1 teaspoon baking powder and omit the baking soda.

"But the little idiot from Lisbon Falls went ahead and married him anyway," she said, laughing, then took her foot off the gas. Here was Patel's Market on the left—Texaco self-serve pumps on clean black asphalt under blinding white lights—and she felt an amazingly strong urge to pull in and grab a pack of cigarettes. Good old Salem Lights. And while she was there, she could get some of those Nissen doughnuts Manda liked, the squash ones, and maybe some HoHos for herself.

LISEY'S STORY

Winter-Squash Doughnut Holes

Makes 36 doughnut holes

Light, crispy, and not too sweet, squash doughnuts are a variation of Maine's famous potato doughnuts, an after-supper treat since the days when we made them from the meal's leftover mashed potatoes.

The Nissen bakery is long gone from Portland now, but I tried my best to re-create their recipe.

2 cups all-purpose flour

2 teaspoons baking powder (see Note)

¼ teaspoon baking soda

1 teaspoon kosher salt

½ teaspoon freshly grated nutmeg

¼ teaspoon ground cloves

1 cup granulated sugar

1 teaspoon ground cinnamon

3 tablespoons unsalted butter, at room temperature

1 egg

1½ teaspoons vanilla extract

¾ cup cold mashed roasted winter squash (such as butternut, acorn, or hubbard; see Note)

¼ cup buttermilk (see "Buttermilk," page 6), at room temperature

Vegetable oil or vegetable shortening for frying

In a medium bowl, whisk together the flour, baking powder, baking soda, salt, nutmeg, and cloves. In a pie plate, combine ½ cup of the sugar with the cinnamon. Set aside.

CONTINUED

In a large bowl using a handheld mixer on high speed, cream the butter and remaining ½ cup sugar until fluffy, 1 minute. Add the egg and vanilla and beat until glossy and pale yellow, 1 minute more. Add the squash and buttermilk and beat until smooth, about 1 minute. Add the flour mixture and mix on medium-low speed until just combined. The dough will be sticky.

On a generously floured work surface, turn out the dough and flip it to coat with flour. Using your hands, gently press the dough into a 1-inch thickness and, using a 1½-inch biscuit cutter, cut into rounds. Gather the scraps, press them out again, and cut more rounds until the dough is used up.

In a Dutch oven or other large, heavy pot over medium-high heat, warm 3 inches of vegetable oil to 360°F. Line a baking sheet with a double layer of paper towels.

Working in small batches, add the dough rounds to the oil and fry, turning once, until puffed and golden brown on both sides, about 2 minutes per side. Monitor the oil and maintain a steady temperature. Using a slotted spoon, transfer the cooked doughnut holes to the prepared baking sheet to drain. When cool enough to handle, toss the doughnut holes in the cinnamon-sugar.

Serve the doughnut holes warm or at room temperature.

Notes

If you prefer, substitute an equal amount of Bakewell Cream for the baking powder and omit the baking soda.

To roast a winter squash, position an oven rack on the middle rung, heat the oven to 375°F, and line a baking sheet with parchment paper. Cut the squash in half through the poles, scoop out the seeds, and arrange flesh-side up on the prepared baking sheet. Roast until the flesh is fork-tender, 30 to 60 minutes, depending on the squash's size and variety. Remove from the oven and set on a wire rack until cool enough to handle. Scoop the flesh into a bowl and discard the skin. Allow the squash to cool completely, about 1 hour.

UNDER THE DOME

Woops

Makes 15 woops

The Amish in Pennsylvania say they made them first, but I say whoopie pies have had a home in Maine for just as long. Marshmallow fluff sandwiched between two dark chocolate cakes makes a treat big enough to share, and one so good, the folks in Dover-Foxtrot, just north of Derry, still celebrate them every year with a festival in June.

Over in Chester's Mill, Vera Appleton never forgave herself for leaving the kids alone, if only for 30 minutes, and I doubt Alice ever ate another whoopie pie for as long as she lived.

2 cups all-purpose flour

½ cup Dutch-processed cocoa powder

1 teaspoon baking soda

1 teaspoon baking powder

1 teaspoon kosher salt

½ cup vegetable shortening

½ cup butter, at room temperature

1 cup granulated sugar

1 egg

2½ teaspoons vanilla extract

1 cup buttermilk (see "Buttermilk," page 6), plus 2 tablespoons

2 cups powdered sugar

2 cups marshmallow fluff

Position the oven racks on the upper-middle rung and the lower-middle rung and heat the oven to 350°F. Line two baking sheets with parchment paper.

In a medium bowl, whisk together the flour, cocoa powder, baking soda, baking powder, and salt.

In a large bowl using a handheld mixer on high speed, cream together ¼ cup of the shortening, ¼ cup of the butter, and the granulated sugar until pale and fluffy, about 2 minutes. Add the egg and 1 teaspoon of the vanilla and beat for 1 minute more.

CONTINUED

Turn the mixer to low speed; add half the flour mixture, then ½ cup of the buttermilk. Repeat with the remaining flour mixture and ½ cup buttermilk. Beat to combine into a batter, stopping to scrape down the sides of the bowl with a rubber spatula as needed.

Spoon 2 tablespoons of the batter at a time onto the prepared baking sheets, about 2 inches apart, to make a total of thirty small cakes. Bake for 12 to 15 minutes, or until the tops are puffed and a toothpick inserted into the center of one of the cakes comes out clean. Transfer to a wire rack and let cool completely.

In a large bowl using a handheld mixer on high speed, blend the remaining ¼ cup shortening, ¼ cup butter, and 1½ teaspoons vanilla with the powdered sugar and marshmallow fluff until smooth. Add the remaining 2 tablespoons buttermilk, 1 tablespoon at a time, if required to bring the filling together.

Spread the flat side of half the cakes with the filling. Top with the remaining cakes to form a sandwich, then wrap individually in wax paper and store in the fridge for up to 5 days.

Blueberry Cheesecake Pie

Makes one 9-inch deep-dish pie

There are still more than 40,000 acres of wild blueberries in Maine; smaller than their high-bushed cousins, they're sweeter, with a whole lot more flavor. It's a shame that Davie Hogan, and the other contestants of the Great Gretna Pie-Eat, put them to such a waste. Can you imagine the mess? But you reap what you sow when you bully someone by calling him "lard-ass."

This recipe takes some time, and it's worth it. Make the pie the day before serving, or start early in the morning to ensure it has lots of time to chill before slicing. If you have any leftovers, store them in the refrigerator for up to 3 days.

1 recipe short crust pastry (see page 231)

8 ounces cream cheese,
at room temperature

¾ cup sour cream

¾ cup granulated sugar

2 eggs

1 teaspoon vanilla extract

1 teaspoon finely grated lemon zest,
plus 1 teaspoon fresh lemon juice

2 teaspoons cornstarch

½ teaspoon kosher salt

¼ cup water

2½ cups fresh or frozen wild blueberries

Position an oven rack on the lower-middle rung and heat the oven to 425°F.

Roll the pastry dough into a 12-inch circle. Transfer to a 9-inch deep-dish pie plate, pressing the dough firmly against the bottom, sides, and top edge. Leaving a ½-inch overhang, trim away the excess dough.

Line the dough with parchment paper or aluminum foil; pour in ½ inch of pie weights, uncooked rice, or dried beans; and bake for 10 minutes. Remove the crust from the oven and lower the temperature to 375°F.

CONTINUED

BLUEBERRY CHEESECAKE PIE, CONTINUED

Pour out the pie weights and discard the parchment. Using a serrated knife, carefully saw away the overhanging crust from the edge of the pie plate for a tidy finish. Return the crust to the oven and bake until the bottom is dry and just starting to brown, 10 to 12 minutes.

In a large bowl using a handheld mixer on medium-high speed, beat together the cream cheese, sour cream, ½ cup of the sugar, the eggs, vanilla, and lemon zest until just blended. Pour into the par-baked crust.

Cover the edges of the crust with strips of foil to prevent excessive browning and bake until the filling is set, but the center still jiggles slightly when moved, 25 to 30 minutes. Let cool for 1 hour at room temperature.

In a medium saucepan, combine the remaining ¼ cup sugar, cornstarch, and salt. Stir in the water and lemon juice, set over medium heat, and cook, stirring constantly, until the mixture is smooth and thickened. Remove from the heat and add the blueberries, tossing to coat evenly. Drain the berries in a colander, reserving the excess glaze.

Spoon the blueberries over the cooled cheesecake, using the reserved glaze to touch up any dry spots. Let cool completely, then refrigerate for at least 3 hours, or up to 2 days.

Cut the cheesecake pie into slices and serve.

"I know The West Wharf," she says, looking amused in spite of her distress. At the counter, Cathy isn't even pretending to read her magazine. This is better than *Redbook*, by far. "How do *you* know I'm not married, or something?"

"No wedding ring," he replies promptly, although he hasn't even looked at her hands yet, not closely, anyway. "Besides, I was just talking about fried clams, cole slaw, and strawberry shortcake, not a lifetime commitment."

DREAMCATCHER

Old-Fashioned Strawberry Shortcake

Makes 8 servings

Grandma only ever assembled this full shortcake for Grandpa's birthday. She baked the biscuit in the morning, then let it cool completely, sliced it in half, and wrapped it up for later. She mixed the berries and sugar together then too. After dinner, she warmed the biscuit in a 250°F oven for 10 minutes while whipping the cream. She finally put it all together, topped with a single candle.

2 quarts fresh strawberries, hulled

1¼ cups granulated sugar

2 teaspoons fresh lemon juice

3 cups all-purpose flour

1 tablespoon Bakewell Cream (see Note)

1½ teaspoons baking soda

1 teaspoon kosher salt

6 tablespoons cold butter

1¼ cups milk

2 cups whipping cream

2 teaspoons vanilla extract

Set aside eight of the reddest, most blemish-free strawberries for the garnish. Slice the remaining strawberries and place in a medium bowl. Sprinkle with 1 cup of the sugar and the lemon juice, stir to combine, cover, and refrigerate for at least 1 hour, or up to overnight.

Position an oven rack on the lower-middle rung and heat the oven to 425°F. Butter an 8-inch round pan.

CONTINUED

In a large bowl, whisk together the flour, Bakewell Cream, baking soda, salt, and 2 tablespoons sugar. Grate the butter into the bowl and, using your fingertips, gently work it into the flour mixture, leaving a few lumps. Make a well in the center, pour in 1 cup plus 3 tablespoons of the milk, and stir to form a soft biscuit dough.

Transfer the dough to a lightly floured work surface and knead three or four times. Pat the dough into the prepared baking pan, brush with the remaining 1 tablespoon milk, and sprinkle with 1 tablespoon sugar. Bake until the top is golden, 30 to 35 minutes. Let cool in the pan for 15 minutes, then remove from the pan and transfer to a wire rack and let cool until just warm.

In a large bowl, using a handheld mixer on high speed, whip the cream to medium peaks. Fold in the vanilla and remaining 1 tablespoon sugar. Let chill in the refrigerator until ready to assemble the shortcake.

Using a serrated knife, gently slice the biscuit in half horizontally, through the middle. Use a 3-inch biscuit cutter to cut a hole in the center of each piece and set the cut-out pieces aside. Place the bottom of the large biscuit on a serving plate. Top with about half of the strawberries and their juice, then a thick layer of whipped cream. Cover with the top half of the large biscuit and spoon about half the remaining strawberries and their juice into the hole in the center. Garnish the top with eight small dollops of whipped cream evenly spaced around the edge, and one large dollop on the strawberries in the center, if desired. Top each small dollop with a reserved strawberry.

Build another smaller shortcake with the cut-out rounds of biscuit and the remaining strawberries and top with a dollop of whipped cream.

Slice and serve the big shortcake, passing the remaining whipped cream at the table. Serve the star of the celebration the individual shortcake; or do what my Grandma did and save it for yourself and your helpers.

Note
No Bakewell Cream? Substitute 1 tablespoon baking powder and omit the baking soda.

The partygoers turned to look at them for a moment—Marie never forgot David's round, solemn eyes—and then turned back to watch Hilly open his magic set.

"I wonder if there's any of that maple-walnut ice cream left," Ev wondered aloud. And Hilly, who that afternoon believed his grandfather to be the greatest man on earth, ran to get it.

THE TOMMYKNOCKERS

Maple-Walnut Ice Cream

Makes 6 servings

A popular flavor across Maine and the rest of New England, my maple-walnut ice cream combines the sweetness of maple syrup with a creamy frozen custard and lots of lightly spiced walnuts.

1 cup maple syrup
1½ cups milk
1½ cups whipping cream
4 egg yolks
1 cup walnut pieces
1 tablespoon butter
¼ teaspoon ground cinnamon
1 pinch cayenne pepper

In a medium saucepan over high heat, boil ¾ cup of the maple syrup until it is reduced to ½ cup, 3 to 5 minutes. Turn the heat to medium-low and stir in the milk and cream.

Place the egg yolks in a medium bowl. Whisking continuously, slowly add 1 cup of the cream mixture into the egg yolks to temper them. Pour everything back into the saucepan and warm over medium-low heat, stirring continuously, until this custard has thickened enough to coat the back of a spoon, and your finger leaves a clear trail when drawn through it, 8 to 10 minutes. Do not leave the pan unattended.

Strain the mixture through a fine-mesh sieve into a medium metal bowl to catch any bits of cooked egg yolk. Set on top of a wire rack or trivet and stir occasionally to cool for 1 hour, then transfer to the refrigerator to cool completely, about 4 hours.

CONTINUED

In a medium skillet over medium heat, toast the walnuts, stirring occasionally, until aromatic and just turning golden, 3 to 5 minutes. Add the remaining ¼ cup maple syrup, the butter, cinnamon, and cayenne. Toss to coat and cook until the syrup has caramelized, 1 to 2 minutes. Transfer to a large plate and separate the nuts from each other to prevent sticking. Let cool completely, about 45 minutes.

Add the custard to an ice-cream maker and churn according to the manufacturer's instructions, adding the walnuts during the last few minutes of churning. Transfer the ice cream to a shallow container, cover, and freeze until firm, 6 to 8 hours.

When ready to serve, allow the ice cream to soften on the counter for 5 to 10 minutes, if necessary, then scoop into bowls or onto cones.

Note

To speed the cooling of the custard, prepare an ice bath by filling a large bowl (or bucket) with ice and cold water. Carefully lower the bowl of custard until it is floating in the ice bath and stir regularly to cool.

Drinks and Cocktails

Now to talk about Derry. I've made no mystery about my thoughts on THAT. DAMN. TOWN. up 'til now, and what went on there is enough to drive a person to drink, even today. Something very old, and very evil, lived down deep, underneath the streets. Call it Pennywise or Bob Gray, It awoke every twenty-seven years or so to feed on the children, devouring their terror and wiping the memories of everyone who should have done something about It.

The storm of '85 is what took out the Standpipe and sent thousands of tons of water from Up-Mile Hill into downtown Derry, sweeping away the Canal's supports and sinking most of the town and many of its people with it. But The Loser's Club put that evil to bed once and for all; in particular Bill Denbrough, who crushed It's heart between his own two hands.

There's most likely no truth in it, but I have wondered over the years if part of the town's forgetfulness isn't due to Maine's favorite spirit, Allen's Coffee Brandy. It's strong stuff at 60 proof, and the *champagne of Maine* is often sipped straight out of the bottle, though hunters and fishermen across the state enjoy it mixed into a jug of milk. Add it to cream, and you've got a Sombrero. Add it to rum with a bit of lemon juice and it's a Moonquake. Careful now, those are deadly.

Allen's also adds a nice kick to a chocolate frappe when you need more than a spoonful of espresso powder to get you up and running. My frappe recipe is Maine all the way, but I played a bit with the ice-cream soda, turning it into a dairy-free blend of strawberry and coconut milk, sweetened with cream soda and maple syrup.

The eggnog, on the other hand, is chock-full of dairy, eggs, and rum. It's a traditional recipe, from back in the day, and is best shared with family and friends at such winter celebrations as Christmas and New Year's Eve.

The recipe for root beer comes from my dad's dad. I gave over the making of it to Ray once he got old enough for the responsibility. That meant keeping the ginger bug alive in the cellar, feeding it with ginger and sugar every week or two, then brewing the beer from barks and roots, adding the bug, and setting it up to ferment until nice and bubbly.

We didn't know it back then, but I've read that, on account of the fermentation, ginger bugs are probiotic, meaning they've got all sorts of wild yeasts and healthy bacteria for our guts and digestion. You can use the ginger bug to ferment almost any fruit juice or tea, as long as it's sweetened. Iced tea is lovely with a few bubbles, and when you ferment homemade sweet-and-sour mix with a ginger bug, the result is probiotic margaritas—healthy may be a stretch—but delicious is not, especially when combined with jalapeño olive brine.

Cheers, my friends. Here's to better times.

"Oh, about beer I never lie," Crandall said. "A man who lies about beer makes enemies. Sit down, Doc. I put an extra couple on ice, just in case."

PET SEMATARY

Mom's Iced Red Tea

Makes 8 cups

I suspect a pitcher of iced tea is a summer staple in most fridges across the country. This recipe comes from Peter Riley's mother and combines red rooibos tea and citrus peels for refreshing, noncaffeinated relief from the heat.

There's nothing like an ice-cold glass of iced tea to welcome you back to the comfort of home, and the shelter it provides from the storms raging outside, even if most of them are of your own making. Lord knows Peter needed it.

6 rooibos tea bags

8 wide strips lemon zest,
plus lemon slices for serving

8 wide strips orange zest,
plus orange slices for serving

4 cups boiling water,
plus 4 cups cold water

Ice cubes for serving

In a large pot, combine the tea bags, lemon zest, orange zest, and boiling water and let steep for 8 to 10 minutes. Remove the tea bags, pour in the cold water, and refrigerate until cooled completely, about 2 hours, or up to 1 week.

When ready to serve, pour the chilled tea into large glasses filled with ice and garnish each with a slice of lemon and a slice of orange.

Variation

For a lightly sweetened and carbonated probiotic version of iced red tea, add ½ cup granulated or cane sugar to the pot with the tea bags and citrus zests. When completely cool, mix the tea with ½ cup Ginger Bug (page 234) and bottle according to the instructions in Homemade Root Beer (facing page).

Tommy suggested they stop at the Kelly Fruit after and grab a root
beer and a burger. All the other kids would be going to Westover or
Lewiston, and they would have the place to themselves. Carrie's face
lit up, he said. She told him that would be fine. Just fine.

This is the girl they keep calling a monster. I want you to keep that
firmly in mind. The girl who could be satisfied with a hamburger and a
dime root beer after her only school dance so her momma wouldn't be
worried. . . .

CARRIE

Homemade Root Beer

Makes about 1 gallon

Poor Carrie White, that girl never did get
to the Kelly Fruit after that fateful school
dance, but a big batch of root beer is always
popular at parties.

This is how my daddy made it, with a ginger
bug. It looks like there's a lot of sugar and
molasses in there, but the ginger bug feeds
on both to produce a carbonated soda with
a lightly sweetened, old-world taste.

1 gallon water
½ cup dried birch bark (see Note)
½ cup dried sassafras bark (see Note)
½ cup dried sarsaparilla root (see Note)
1 star anise pod
1 cup granulated sugar
½ cup molasses
1 vanilla pod, split lengthwise
1 cup Ginger Bug (page 234), including
1 tablespoon ginger pieces from the
bottom of the jar

In a stockpot over high heat, combine the water,
birch bark, sassafras bark, sarsaparilla root, and
star anise and bring to a boil. Turn the heat to
medium-low and simmer for 20 minutes, then
remove the pot from the heat and stir in the sugar,
molasses, and vanilla pod. Let cool completely.

Strain the mixture into a wide-mouth 1-gallon jar
and stir in the ginger bug, including the ginger
pieces. Cover with a paper towel or coffee filter
and secure in place with a rubber band or jar ring.

CONTINUED

Place the jar somewhere warm and dark, such as a cupboard, to ferment, and stir once per day. When it starts to bubble, after 3 to 5 days, it is ready to bottle.

Set a small strainer over a funnel to catch the vanilla pod and ginger and strain the root beer into flip-top glass or plastic bottles. Make sure to leave an inch or two of headspace at the top of each bottle. Cap the bottles and set aside in a quiet corner at room temperature for about 1 week to build up carbonation. After that, transfer the bottles to the refrigerator to slow the carbonation process and avoid explosions.

Homemade root beer is best consumed within 1 month of bottling.

Note

Look for the birch bark, sassafras bark, and sarsaparilla root in your local natural foods store, or order them online.

```
"Have you read the new one?"

"Billy Said Keep Going? Not yet. Miss Coogan at the drugstore says
it's pretty racy."

"Hell, it's almost puritanical," Ben said. "The language is rough, but
when you're writing about uneducated country boys, you can't . . .
look, can I buy you an ice-cream soda or something? I was just getting
a hanker on for one."

She checked his eyes a third time. Then smiled, warmly. "Sure. I'd
love one. They're great in Spencer's."

That was the beginning of it.
                        ─────────────
                        'SALEM'S LOT
```

Strawberry-Coconut Cream Soda

Makes 2 servings

If you're thinking about visiting Spencer's in 'Salem's Lot, go careful. The town may have burned, but the undead live on. Still, there's no more romantic a vision than a pair of budding lovebirds sharing an ice-cream soda on a first date. Shame it's not something you see anymore.

This coconut cream is a vegan version, but just as delicious and refreshing.

2 cups frozen strawberries
One 13.5-ounce can coconut milk
8 ounces cream soda, or as needed
1 tablespoon maple syrup

In a blender, combine the strawberries, coconut milk, cream soda, and maple syrup. Blend on high speed until smooth and creamy, scraping down the sides as necessary, about 1 minute. Thin with more cream soda, if desired, and re-blend.

Pour the soda into two tall glasses and enjoy.

"Moogy." [Lois] tossed her hair pertly. "That's a word I made up to describe how Mr. Chasse looked when he was pretending to listen to me but was actually thinking about his coin collection. I know a moogy look when I see one, Ralph. What are you thinking about?"

"I was wondering what time you think you'll get back from your card-game."

"That depends."

"On what?"

"On whether or not we stop at Tubby's for chocolate frappes."

INSOMNIA

Tubby's Super-Charged Chocolate Frappe

Makes 1 serving

In Maine, a milkshake has milk and flavored syrup. If you want ice cream, then ask for a frappe. Tubby's signature frappe had a spoonful of instant coffee in it for an extra kick.

I'm sure Lois Chasse and her girlfriends over in Derry never considered it, but I'll bet that more than a few customers livened theirs up with a shot or two of Allen's Coffee Brandy.

2 cups chocolate ice cream

½ cup milk

2 tablespoons chocolate syrup

1 teaspoon instant espresso powder, or 1 ounce coffee brandy (such as Allen's)

1 tablespoon grated semisweet chocolate

In a blender, combine the ice cream, milk, chocolate syrup, and espresso powder. Blend until smooth and frothy, about 1 minute.

Pour the frappe into a tall glass, garnish with the grated chocolate, and serve.

Later on, while we were doing a final polish on the kitchen (and sipping eggnog), I asked her if she remembered why we used to call the Bale Road Bridge the Fail Road Bridge. She cocked her head and laughed.

"It was your old friend who thought that up. The one I had such a crush on."

"Charlie Keen," I said. "I haven't seen him in a dog's age. Except on TV. The poor man's Sanjay Gupta."

"N."

Fail Road Eggnog

Makes 8 servings

This one goes back generations; most families I know all have their own recipes similar to this one. It's got a shed load of booze in it, so I doubt anyone will be serving it to a pregnant woman; still, there's raw egg whites in this traditional recipe, so don't serve it to anyone who is immunocompromised.

3 cups milk

6 eggs, separated

¾ cup granulated sugar

1 cup whipping cream

1½ cups dark rum

¼ cup bourbon

Freshly grated nutmeg for serving

Prepare an ice bath by filling a large bowl (or bucket) with ice and cold water.

In a large saucepan over medium heat, warm 2 cups of the milk until steaming, but do not allow it to boil. Turn off the heat.

In a medium metal or ceramic bowl, whisk the egg yolks with ½ cup of the sugar until pale and thick. Whisking continuously, add 1 cup of the warm milk to the yolks. Pour this mixture back into the pan, turn the heat to medium-low, and cook, stirring continuously, until this custard has thickened enough to coat the back of a spoon, and your finger leaves a clear trail when drawn through it. Do not leave the pan unattended. Clean and dry the bowl.

Stir the cream into the mixture and then strain into the medium bowl; place in the prepared ice bath and stir occasionally to cool completely. Pour into a punch bowl and stir in the rum, bourbon, and remaining 1 cup milk.

In a large bowl, using a handheld mixer on high speed, beat the egg whites with the remaining ¼ cup sugar to form soft peaks. Fold the egg whites into the eggnog, transfer to the fridge, and let chill thoroughly. Whisk to re-blend and then serve topped with a grating of nutmeg.

"A GOOD MARRIAGE"

The Lighthouse Margarita

Makes 4 large servings

This delicious mixture of sweet and salty has a bit of a kick. The secret to it, jalapeño olive brine, will keep your friends guessing. Never tell; a little doubt is all you need to keep a good secret.

Another secret? It's easy to get away with the murder of a murderer, especially when the police seem to think you did the right thing. Darcy Anderson knows.

Kosher or coarse salt

1 lime, cut into 5 wedges

Ice cubes for mixing

8 ounces reposado tequila

4 ounces Grand Marnier

4 ounces fresh lime juice

2 cups sweet and sour mix (see page 218)

2 ounces jalapeño-stuffed olive brine, plus 4 olives

Pour a layer of salt onto a small plate. Using 1 lime wedge, wet a half lip on four margarita glasses and then dip them in the salt. Put the glasses in the fridge to chill.

In a pitcher half-filled with ice, combine the tequila, Grand Marnier, lime juice, sweet and sour mix, and olive brine and stir vigorously for 10 seconds. Strain into the prepared glasses. Combine 1 lime wedge and 1 olive on each of four cocktail spears.

Serve the margaritas immediately, garnished with the olive–lime wedge spears.

Sweet and Sour Mix

Makes about 6 cups

Use this to make The Lighthouse Margarita, or any other cocktail that uses sweet and sour mix, like a whisky sour, cosmopolitan, or sidecar.

2 cups water
2 cups granulated sugar
1½ cups fresh lime juice
1 cup fresh lemon juice

In a large saucepan over medium-high heat, combine the water and sugar and bring to a boil, stirring occasionally. Let boil for 1 minute, then remove this syrup from the heat and let cool for 15 minutes.

In a large pitcher, combine the syrup with the lime juice and lemon juice and mix well. Refrigerate until cool.

Store the mix in the fridge for up to 1 week.

Variation
For lightly carbonated, probiotic drinks, stir ½ cup Ginger Bug (page 234) into the cooled sweet and sour mix and bottle according to the instructions in Homemade Root Beer (page 209).

"Yes, madame," the waiter said, licking his lips. People were
looking at them. A few smiled . . . but those who got a look at
Anne Anderson's eyes soon stopped. The waiter started away and
she called him back, her voice loud and even and undeniable.

"A sombrero," she said, "has Kahlua and cream in it. Cream.
If you bring me a sombrero with milk in it, chum, you're going
to be shampooing with the motherfucker."

THE TOMMYKNOCKERS

MoFo Sombrero

Makes 1 serving

Anne Anderson sounds like she was a handful, but as a born-and-bred Mainer, I share her passion about the importance of cream in a sombrero.

We disagree about the Kahlua, though. Only Allen's Coffee Brandy will do for me. But if Kahlua is all you can get, I guess it'll have to do.

2 or 3 ice cubes

2 ounces coffee brandy (such as Allen's)
or coffee liqueur (such as Kahlua)

3 ounces light cream or half-and-half

Put the ice in an old-fashioned glass. Add the coffee brandy, then pour the cream over top. Do not stir.

Garnish the sombrero with a stir stick and serve.

Note
Vanilla soy milk or almond milk makes a tasty dairy-free alternative to the cream—don't tell Anne that I said so.

"I won't even ask why you had your stove going on a hot July night, because after thirty years in the policing business, I know drunks are apt to take any half-baked notion into their heads. Would you agree with that?"

"Well . . . ayuh," Alden admitted. "Drunks are unpredictable. And those Moonquakes are deadly."

"Which is why your cabin out there on Abenaki Lake is now burning to the ground."

"Jesus Christ on a crutch!"

"DRUNKEN FIREWORKS"

Deadly Moonquake

Makes 1 serving

Crazy old Alden McCausland wasn't much after his mama died. He kept the money she won on that Big Maine Millions scratcher, sure, but he never did have half her brains. Lucky for him, she lived long enough to make that deal with the Massimos; it left their cabin in ashes, but kept him out of jail.

A night of moonquakes can set your whole life ablaze. Imbibe with caution.

Ice cubes for shaking
1½ ounces dark rum
1 ounce coffee brandy (such as Allen's)
½ ounce fresh lemon juice

Fill a cocktail shaker with ice. Add the rum, coffee brandy, and lemon juice and shake for 10 seconds.

Strain the moonquake into a martini glass and serve.

Basics

I've just about talked myself out, but there's a bit left to say about these basic recipes. They're all here in one place because I know you'll flip back to them again and again.

They come from far and wide. The red sauce from Gambino's in Derry, the fry mix and cocktail sauce from my first job in that fish shack off Freeport. The pastry is my grannie's recipe, and the pasta dough and corn tortilla recipes I got from Missy Donaldson at Holy Frijole in Castle Rock. The tartar sauce and French dressing are modern ones of my own making, inspired by recipes from the past.

While the dressing, sauces, and fry mix are fast and easy, others can be trickier to master. The corn tortillas, short crust pastry, and pasta dough will get better every time you make them, as you learn how wet (or dry) each of the doughs should be, and how to tell when the dough is ready to be rolled or pressed out. Hell is repetition, as André Linoge was heard to say, but not all repetition is hell. It is the mastery of foundational recipes such as these that makes you a great cook.

The final recipe, for a ginger bug, can be the most finicky of all. Wild yeast is no match for the sterile environments of modern grocery stores, so finding organic ginger that will result in a lively bug can be a challenge. Look for organic ginger, or turmeric, from a farmers' market, or better yet, grow your own if you're in the climate to do it.

Take it from this seasoned survivor: the less you rely on the Major for the basics, the better off you'll be.

The cop sat in the car while Thad went in. He got his soda and was inspecting the wild array of dips (you had your basic clam, and if you didn't like that, you had your basic onion) when the telephone rang.

THE DARK HALF

New England Fry Mix

Makes 2 cups

This classic seafood-shack mix produces crispy fried shellfish and battered fish. Use it in Lobster Pickin's (page 95), Fried Clam Rolls (page 107), and Moose-Lickit Fish and Chips (page 117).

1 cup 00 durum flour or all-purpose flour (see "Flour," page 6)
1 cup yellow corn flour or masa harina (see Note)
2 teaspoons table salt or fine sea salt
½ teaspoon finely ground black pepper

In a large bowl, whisk together the 00 flour, corn flour, salt, and pepper.

Store the fry mix in a covered container at room temperature for up to 3 months.

Note
Corn flour is neither cornstarch nor cornmeal. It is ground from the entire dried kernel of corn and is a similar texture to whole-wheat flour. If you can't find it, masa harina makes a good substitute.

Tarragon Tartar Sauce

Makes about 1 cup

A variation on classic tartar sauce, flavored with tarragon and white wine vinegar. Delicious alongside Lobster Pickin's (page 95), Fried Clam Rolls (page 107), and Moose-Lickit Fish and Chips (page 117).

½ cup dry white wine
¼ cup white wine vinegar
½ cup minced shallot
6 teaspoons minced tarragon leaves, or 2 teaspoons dried tarragon
¾ cup mayonnaise
Kosher salt

In a small saucepan over medium-high heat, combine the wine and vinegar. Add the shallot and 4 teaspoons of the tarragon (1½ teaspoons dried) and bring to a boil. Let boil, stirring occasionally, until reduced to 1 tablespoon of liquid, 5 to 7 minutes. Transfer to a shallow bowl, set on a wire rack, and let cool for 15 minutes, then stir in the mayonnaise and remaining 2 teaspoons tarragon (½ teaspoon dried). Taste and season with salt. Transfer to the refrigerator and let chill.

Store the tartar sauce in the refrigerator for up to 1 week.

Smoky Cocktail Sauce

Makes 1¼ cups

A classic cocktail sauce with a hint of smoke and a dash of heat. Serve with Lobster Pickin's (page 95), Fried Clam Rolls (page 107), or your favorite fish and shellfish.

1 cup ketchup
¼ cup prepared horseradish
1 teaspoon fresh lemon juice
½ teaspoon Worcestershire sauce
¼ teaspoon smoked paprika
2 or 3 dashes hot sauce (such as Louisiana or Tabasco)

In a small bowl, combine the ketchup, horseradish, lemon juice, Worcestershire, paprika, and hot sauce. Stir well and transfer to the refrigerator to chill.

Store the cocktail sauce in the refrigerator for up to 1 week.

Italian Red Sauce

Makes about 3 cups

An easy and surprisingly delicious uncooked tomato sauce used in Sausage Pizza from Gambino's (page 71) and Nettie's Rolled Lasagna (page 133).

One 28-ounce can quality crushed tomatoes (see Note, page 82)
2 tablespoons olive oil
1 garlic clove, grated or minced
1 teaspoon kosher salt

In a medium bowl, combine the tomatoes, olive oil, garlic, and salt. Stir well and set aside on the counter for 1 hour to allow the flavors to marry before using.

Store the red sauce in the refrigerator for up to 5 days.

Nouveau French Dressing

Makes about 1 cup

A twenty-first-century, low-sugar version of the classic '70s bottled vinaigrette. Versatile beyond just a bowl of greens, use it in Ben's Really Big Salad (page 37), Gramma's Crab Cake Brunch (page 29), and Blue Cheese Broccoli (page 159).

¼ cup coarsely chopped shallot
¼ cup red wine vinegar
¼ cup olive oil
¼ cup vegetable oil
2 teaspoons tomato paste
1 teaspoon Dijon mustard
1 teaspoon granulated sugar
Kosher salt
Freshly ground black pepper

In the bowl of a small food processor, combine the shallot and vinegar. Pulse four or five times and allow to sit for 15 minutes. Add the olive oil, vegetable oil, tomato paste, mustard, sugar, ½ teaspoon salt, and a pinch of pepper and process until pureed. Taste and season with more salt and pepper if needed. Transfer to a jar or small bowl.

Store the dressing in the refrigerator for up to 1 week. Shake or whisk to recombine before serving.

Yellow Corn Tortillas

Makes twelve 6-inch tortillas

Masa harina is flour, ground from dried corn kernels that have been cooked and soaked in limewater. Use these tortillas in Holy Frijole Enchiladas (page 147) or as a taco-style alternative to Fried Clam Rolls (page 107), or serve with Vegan Chili at Jon's (page 130).

2 cups masa harina
½ teaspoon table salt or fine sea salt
1½ to 2 cups hot water

In a large bowl, stir together the masa harina and salt. Gradually add enough of the water, mixing with your hands, until the dough is firm and springs back when poked. It should be neither dry nor sticky. Cover the bowl with a clean dish towel and then a plate and allow the dough to rest at room temperature for 1 hour.

Divide the dough into twelve 2-ounce balls. Cover with a clean, damp dish towel.

Warm a large cast-iron pan or griddle over medium-low heat. Cut two 6-inch squares of parchment paper. Place a dough ball between the squares of parchment paper and, using a tortilla press or the bottom of a heavy cast-iron pan, flatten the dough into a 6-inch disc.

Turn the heat under the pan to medium-high, add the tortilla, and cook until the top dries out and the bottom is browned, about 1 minute. Flip and cook for about 30 seconds more to brown the other side. Wrap in a clean dish towel to keep warm.

Repeat with the remaining dough, alternately flattening and cooking the dough, lowering the heat as necessary to prevent scorching, and stacking the tortillas together in the clean dish towel.

Serve the tortillas warm.

Short Crust Pastry

Makes one 9- to 12-inch piecrust

A tried-and-true, no-fuss piecrust recipe used in Blueberry Cheesecake Pie (page 195). To make a homemade two-crust pie for Rotisserie Chicken Pie (page 68), double all the ingredients, except for the egg yolk—one is sufficient.

1¼ cups all-purpose flour
1 teaspoon granulated sugar
½ teaspoon kosher salt
½ cup cold butter
3 to 4 tablespoons ice water
1 egg yolk
½ teaspoon fresh lemon juice or vinegar

In a large bowl, stir together the flour, sugar, and salt. Grate the butter into the bowl and, using your fingertips, gently work it into the flour mixture until you have pea-size lumps and the flour is the color of cornmeal. Make a well in the center of the mixture. In a small bowl, whisk together 3 tablespoons of the ice water, the egg yolk, and lemon juice. Pour the liquid mixture into the well and use your fingertips to bring the dough together into a shaggy ball.

Transfer the dough and any loose flour from your bowl onto the counter and knead quickly and lightly into a ball, adding the remaining ice water 1 teaspoon at a time if needed to bring the dough together.

Divide the dough in half and form into two 1-inch-thick discs. Wrap tightly in plastic wrap and refrigerate for at least 30 minutes, or store in the fridge for up to 2 days or in the freezer for up to 1 month. (If the dough is chilled for more than 30 minutes, it will have to rest on the counter for about 15 minutes before it's soft enough to roll.)

On a lightly floured work surface, using a rolling pin and even pressure, roll the dough out from the center in all four compass directions: north, south, east, and west. Turn and loosen the dough occasionally as you continue to roll it into a circle that is an even ⅛ inch thick (unless otherwise directed in the recipe). Cut out shapes as directed, or roll the dough lightly up onto the rolling pin and transfer to a pie dish.

Fresh Pasta Dough

Makes four 5-ounce servings

A basic dough used to make fresh pasta for Fettuccini Alfredo (page 132) and Nettie's Rolled Lasagna (page 133). If you prefer to make the dough ahead of time, wrap it tightly in wax paper or plastic wrap and refrigerate for up to 24 hours. Remove it from the fridge about 30 minutes before rolling.

3 cups 00 durum flour or all-purpose flour, plus more for dusting
4 eggs, beaten (see Note)
1 tablespoon olive oil

Put the flour in a large bowl and make a well in the center. Pour the beaten eggs into the well, add the olive oil, and, using the fingertips of one hand, gradually bring the flour around the edges into the egg mixture to form a smooth, firm dough that is not sticky. Transfer to a clean work surface and knead for 2 to 3 minutes.

Divide the dough into two equal pieces, form into discs about 1 inch thick, and wrap tightly with wax paper or plastic wrap. Let rest on the counter for at least 30 minutes, or up to 4 hours, before rolling.

Divide one disc of pasta dough into three pieces, flatten them to ½ inch thick, and keep two pieces covered while you roll out the other. Set the pasta roller to its widest setting and feed the dough through. Fold the resulting sheet of pasta crosswise into thirds and then feed it through the rollers again, still on the widest setting. Repeat another one or two times until the sheet is silky smooth.

Lower the thickness setting by one and pass the sheet through the roller again. Repeat, lowering the thickness setting one at a time, until the pasta achieves the desired thickness; for lasagna and fettuccini, the second to last setting; for filled pastas, the last, or narrowest, setting. Dust the pasta with flour to prevent sticking, fold loosely in half crosswise, and lay on a clean dish towel. Repeat with the remaining pasta dough.

For lasagna, cut each sheet into 10- to 12-inch lengths, and use as directed in the recipe.

For fettuccini, line a baking sheet with a clean dish towel. Run the floured sheets through a pasta cutter or cut them by hand. On a floured cutting board, fold both ends of a sheet into the middle, gently fold one side on top of the other, and, using a sharp knife, cut the dough lengthwise through the folds, into ¼-inch slices. Immediately unravel the slices to reveal the pasta ribbons, dust with a little more flour, and twist into loose nests. Arrange the pasta ribbons on the prepared baking sheet and repeat with the remaining sheets of pasta.

Note
Eggs, even when they're all labeled "large," can vary in size. If your dough is too dry, add a tablespoon or two of water, a teaspoon at a time, to bring it together.

Quick Chicken Stock

Makes about 8 cups

Make the most of every bird and bone—
homemade chicken stock is lower in salt
and bigger in taste than store-bought. Use
it in Better-than-Canned Mulligatawny
(page 41), Rotisserie Chicken Pie (page 68),
the Blue Plate Special (page 65), and more.

To save time, collect two or three carcasses
in the freezer and make a big batch of stock
all in one go.

1 rotisserie chicken carcass, picked clean
of meat and skin (see Notes)

8 cups cold water

1 small yellow onion, quartered

1 garlic clove, halved

2 pieces dried mushroom (such as porcini
or morel; optional)

2 thyme sprigs

6 black peppercorns

1-inch strip lemon peel

In a large pot over medium-high heat, combine
the chicken carcass and water and bring to a boil.
Turn the heat to medium-low and add the onion,
garlic, dried mushroom (if using), thyme, peppercorns, and lemon peel. Simmer for 45 minutes to
1 hour, skimming the surface of the stock occasionally to remove fat and other impurities.

Ladle the stock from the pot and strain into a
glass or metal bowl. Use immediately or place the
bowl on a wire rack and let cool for 30 minutes.

Store the stock, covered, in the fridge for up to
3 days, or in the freezer for up to 1 month.

Notes

The cleaner you pick the carcass of meat and
skin, the clearer, and less cloudy, your stock
will be.

Because rotisserie chickens are cooked, self-
basting, for hours, the bones are soft and full
of flavor. If you use a home-roasted chicken or
raw bones to make stock, increase the simmer
time to 2 to 3 hours.

Ginger Bug

Makes 3 cups

An old-fashioned fermentation method used to naturally carbonate traditional beverages such as ginger beer and Homemade Root Beer (page 209). Use it to make a bubbly batch of Mom's Iced Red Tea (page 208), or to ferment the sweet and sour mix for a probiotic version of The Lighthouse Margarita (page 217).

Avoid alternative sweeteners; a ginger bug needs a caloric sweetener (sucrose) to feed. Unrefined organic cane sugar is my preferred choice for a dark, richly colored root beer, but you can also make a pale-colored bug using granulated sugar.

3 cups filtered, chlorine-free water, at room temperature
5 tablespoons cane sugar, or as needed
1½ ounces unpeeled fresh ginger (preferably organic, see Note), or as needed

In a 1-quart canning jar, combine the water with 3 tablespoons of the sugar. Coarsely grate 3 tablespoons of the ginger, add it to the jar, and stir until the sugar is dissolved. Cover with a paper towel or coffee filter and secure in place with a rubber band or jar ring.

Place the jar somewhere warm and dark, such as a cupboard, to ferment, and stir once per day. It will begin to smell yeasty, like bread dough or beer, which is normal. A small amount of scum may form on the top, which is also normal. If you see mold, or it smells rotten, discard the bug and start again. (See Note.)

In three or four days, the bug will start to foam and bubble. On the fourth day, grate another 1 tablespoon ginger and feed it to the bug with 1 tablespoon sugar. On the fifth day, stir in another 1 tablespoon grated ginger and the remaining 1 tablespoon sugar.

When the bug becomes very bubbly, it's ready to make your favorite carbonated soda or beverage, usually somewhere between Day Five and Day Seven.

Store the bug in the fridge and feed it once a week by stirring in 1 tablespoon freshly grated ginger and 1 teaspoon sugar until you are ready to make soda. To replenish the bug after removing ½ to 1 cup to make soda, feed it 1 tablespoon freshly grated ginger, 1 tablespoon sugar, and ½ to 1 cup water.

Notes
Use only organic, unpeeled ginger; conventionally grown ginger is likely irradiated, a process that sterilizes the wild bacteria and yeasts needed for fermentation. Fresh organic turmeric can be substituted for the ginger, to produce a bright yellow bug.

If your bug failed, ensure your water is chlorine-free by leaving it uncovered on the counter overnight, and that your storage area is warm enough to encourage fermentation. If the bug is free of mold but not bubbly after 7 days, bottle it in a flip-top glass or plastic bottle and leave it for 24 hours. It may carbonate better once capped. If not, discard and start again, using ginger from a different source, if possible.

AFTERWORD

Writing a fictional cookbook begins with reading. Constantly, nonstop, for weeks. I'll be honest; it's not terrible, especially for someone who, as a kid, always had a book on her, just in case there was time to get in another chapter when no one was looking. In the case of *Castle Rock Kitchen*, Stephen King's library kept me busy reading for six months solid and then, intermittently, for another two years while the project came together.

I had read many of his stories over the years, but this time I read them in the order in which they were published. Every mention of food on my e-reader got highlighted along the way. It was a slow and worrying start. *Carrie* contains a brief mention of hamburgers and a root beer after the prom, and that's it. *'Salem's Lot* was much more hopeful—hah!—there are ice-cream sodas, spaghetti sauce, pork chops, and more. Then there is Jack Torrance's terrifying bar full of cocktails in *The Shining*, juxtaposed against the comfort of Wendy's Thanksgiving turkey and Dick Hallorann's baked beans.

Eventually, by *Elevation*, published in 2018, the food had transformed from mostly down-home Maine favorites to include gourmet vegetarian Mexican food. Along the way, I found canapés in *Pet Sematary*, cheese fondue in *Needful Things*, Lobster Pickin's in *11/22/63*, and that was just the beginning.

I found inspiration in the dishes that King describes directly in the text, especially when the passages are ripe with poignancy, such as Homemade Root Beer from *Carrie*, or rich with humor, like Pancakes with the Toziers from *It*. Food brings people, and characters, together; countless issues in real life, and on the pages, get sorted out around a table filled with food and drink.

The title for the most creative recipe goes to Interstellar Escargot from "The Body." Forty years after King imagined them, those snails presented me with my biggest recipe challenge since the Turtle Soup in *Outlander Kitchen I*. I also looked for passages that use food to describe a character, or as a metaphor. Those are some of my favorites and include Gramma's Crab Cake Brunch and Dolores's Oven Risotto.

The titles of the dishes may appear in the pages of Stephen King's books, but my recipes come from Maine tradition. They're also influenced by the family traditions that I learned while standing on a stool beside my mother and grandmothers in their kitchens, as well as my own experience as a professionally trained cook.

It's a crazy, creative time, generating the framework for a cookbook based on fiction. Ideas come all day, and night, and the (color-coded) spreadsheet that I use to keep everything organized changes hourly until the whirlwind slows and I finally settle on a first draft of the table of contents. That first draft included dishes from almost all of Stephen King's books, including *The Stand*, *The Dark Tower* series, *The Talisman*, *The Green Mile*, *Doctor Sleep*, and *The Outsider*.

After I got Mr. King's go-ahead and found a publisher in Ten Speed Press, we narrowed the focus of the cookbook to include only his stories set in Maine, which is more than forty by my count in the Bibliography. That meant I had to leave some of his classics behind, at least for now.

At the same time, it focused the contents on the food of Maine. The state has a long and proud food history; the first Europeans arrived four hundred years ago to fish, and Maine's first cannery opened in the mid-nineteenth century when sardines were a luxury food and lobsters were for prisoners and the poor. In addition to the ocean's bounty, Maine's agricultural production is also significant: blueberries, potatoes, cranberries, apples, maple syrup, poultry, and more.

Born and raised on the opposite coast, in Vancouver, BC, Canada, and now living on a small island between Vancouver and Victoria, I must confess that I've been to Maine only once. That was back in 2008, a year after the death of my father. I joined a silent retreat where I gave myself the space to look forward after months of grief and remembrance. The six days that I spent at Rolling Meadows, southwest of Bangor, changed my life. Three days after my return to my home on Pender Island, I was enrolled in culinary school in Vancouver and packing again, this time for a six-month stay with my mom in her new apartment.

Fourteen years on, I am the author of two *Outlander Kitchen* cookbooks, inspired by the *Outlander* series by Diana Gabaldon, and have completed this, my third fiction-inspired collection of recipes. I've wanted to return to Maine ever since. I had booked my plane tickets and rental car for a planned research trip starting in Bangor in June 2020 when the COVID-19 pandemic hit us full force in March. It wasn't meant to be.

Even without the physical trip, the process of creating, researching, and writing *Castle Rock Kitchen* has been a fulfilling journey, one I am extremely fortunate to have had to keep my mind busy during the months of lockdown.

Pandemic writing on a small island means no nonessential ferry trips to get groceries. Pender has a decent grocery for our twenty-five hundred residents, and the majority of ingredients came from there. The rest, like Bakewell Cream and lobsters from Maine, and Chinese rock sugar, I found online. So will you, if you're unable to source them in your local superstores, groceries, and markets.

To create a fully immersive Castle Rock experience, I developed an alter ego in the character of Mrs. Garraty, but, of course, my own voice creeps in there too. I was born in the big city and lived there for thirty-three years before my husband and I moved to Pender Island. After eighteen years here, I've got a lot of small-town living under my belt and am comfortable with the sense of isolation that comes with life surrounded by the sea. It makes for close neighbors and, I'll admit, a wariness of strangers. A little bit like living in a Stephen King story.

—Theresa Carle-Sanders

BIBLIOGRAPHY

A lot of reading goes into writing a collection of fiction-inspired recipes. Following is a list of the cookbooks, magazines, and websites that I used to learn more about the foodways and traditions of Maine, followed by all of the Stephen King works I read to create this cookbook. To round out my research, I immersed myself in Stephen King's Maine by extensively accessing both the Stephen King official website and the Stephen King Wiki.

Maine

"Agricultural and Seafood Marketing Cookbooks," Digital Maine Repository. Accessed November 2020 through May 2021. https://digitalmaine.com/food_marketing.

Dojny, Brooke. *Dishing Up Maine: 165 Recipes That Capture Authentic Down East Flavors.* North Adams, MA: Storey Publishing, 2006.

Down East: The Magazine of Maine. April 2019: The Maine Food Issue, July 2019: Best of Maine, January 2020: The Way Things Were, April 2020: Back to the Land. Down East Enterprise.

Fender, Don, and Egan, Joseph. (reprint edition). *Lost on a Mountain in Maine.* New York: HarperCollins, 2013.

"Food Section," New England Today. Accessed November 2020 through May 2021. https://newengland.com/category/food.

"Foodways Research: A Taste of Maine," Maine Folklife Center, University of Maine. Accessed November 2020. https://umaine.edu/folklife/what-we-do/exhibits/foodways-research-a-taste-of-maine.

French, Erin. *The Lost Kitchen: Recipes and a Good Life Found in Freedom, Maine.* New York: Clarkson Potter, 2017.

Oliver, Sandra. *Maine Home Cooking: 175 Recipes from Down East Kitchens.* Guilford, CT: Down East Books, 2012.

Standish, Marjorie. *Cooking Down East: Favorite Maine Recipes.* Augusta, ME: Guy Gannett Publishing Company, 1969.

Stephen King

NOVELS

11/22/63

Bag of Bones

Carrie

*Cell**

The Colorado Kid

Cujo

The Cycle of the Werewolf

*The Dark Half**

The Dead Zone

Dolores Claiborne

Dreamcatcher

Elevation

Gerald's Game

*The Girl Who Loved Tom Gordon**

Insomnia

The Institute

It

Lisey's Story

The Long Walk

Needful Things

Pet Sematary

Revival

'Salem's Lot

The Shining

The Tommyknockers

Under the Dome

SHORT STORIES

"The Body"

"Drunken Fireworks"

"Fair Extension"

"A Good Marriage"

"Gramma"

"Graveyard Shift"*

"Gray Matter"

"Hearts in Atlantis"

"It Grows on You"*

"Jerusalem's Lot"*

"The Ledge"*

"The Man in the Black Suit"

"The Mist"

"Mrs. Todd's Shortcut"*

"N."

"Nona"*

"One for the Road"*

"Rita Hayworth and Shawshank Redemption"

"The Sun Dog"

"Uncle Otto's Truck"*

SCREENPLAYS

*The Storm of the Century**

WEBSITES

Stephen King: The Official Website.
Accessed July 2019 to July 2021.
https://stephenking.com/works.

Stephen King Wiki. Accessed
September 2020 to July 2021.
https://stephenking.fandom.com.

* No recipes from the story are included
in the cookbook.

ACKNOWLEDGMENTS

First and foremost, my gratitude to Stephen King for saying yes. Thank you for your generosity with your work and your time.

Howard Sanders, my husband. I'm grateful for your quiet wisdom and advice, and I know our next twenty-six years will be filled with just as much love and adventure.

Susan Finesman, my agent. You arrived in my inbox seven years ago like a fairy godmother, just when I needed you most. There wouldn't be a *Castle Rock Kitchen* without you. Thank you, always, for your guidance and listening ear.

My book team at Ten Speed Press: Shaida Boroumand, Jane Chinn, Stephanie Davis, Sohayla Farman, Mari Gill, David Hawk, Dan Myers, Doug Ogan, and Betsy Stromberg. This book is beyond what I could have dreamed thanks to your input and expertise.

Photographer Jenny Bravo, stylist Chantal Lambeth, and your teams. I am beyond awed by your skills in bringing this book to life visually.

Kate Forest, my friend for over ten years and my virtual assistant for the past couple. You took a huge load off my shoulders so that I could write this book. You are an incredible teammate and friend.

The *Castle Rock Kitchen* recipe testers and their families, a few of whom have childhood or family connections to Maine: Becky and Dave Inbody, Anna and Alan Lapping, Lee Ann Monat, Brianne Begley and Richie Wyckoff, Rhiannon McVean, Jan Anderson and Willie Pung, Jennifer Broughton, Darcy and Jay Gagne, Sue Russo Rogers, Helen Bullard, Jason and Jen Davis, and Lori and John Zachary.

Rachel Lenkowski, the photographer of the first images for *Castle Rock Kitchen*. I will always remember your help and enthusiasm.

The Coven, an extraordinary group of women, some of whom have already been mentioned here. We've proved over the last decade that the thirteen of us can love and support each other through anything.

ABOUT THE CONTRIBUTORS

Photo by Theresa Carle-Sanders

Theresa Carle-Sanders is a trained cook and recipe writer born and raised in Vancouver, British Columbia. After a brief career in corporate management, Theresa went back to culinary school, where she finished at the top of her class. She now combines a lifelong devotion to food and books to create cookbooks inspired by fiction, including *Outlander Kitchen: The Official Outlander Companion Cookbook* and *Outlander Kitchen: To the New World and Back Again*. After living on Pender Island, British Columbia, for eighteen years, Theresa recently moved with her husband, Howard, and their cowboy corgi, Douglas, across the country to New Brunswick.

Stephen King probably wrote the first book you ever read that kept you awake at night. He'll be the first to tell you that fueling nightmares works up quite an appetite, and it's essential to keep an author well fed. Fortunately, these story-inspired recipes feed both hunger and imagination.

Jenny Bravo is a food photographer and production studio owner in Portland, Maine. Having started her career out of culinary school as a private chef before transitioning to photography, Jenny is passionate about capturing food stories. When Jenny is not behind her camera or in her studio kitchen, she is antiquing for her online home decor store, Viand Vintage & Co. She loves spending time with her husband and two young daughters along the beautiful beaches of Maine.

INDEX

Index

Typefaces: Luzi Type's Messina Serif by Luzi Gantenbein, ITC Font's Friz Quadrata Std
by Ernst Friz, Lineto's Akkurat Pro by Laurenz Brunner, Vintage Type's Typewriter

Library of Congress Cataloging-in-Publication Data
    Names: Carle-Sanders, Theresa, author.
    Title: Castle Rock kitchen : wicked good recipes from the world of Stephen King /
        Theresa Carle-Sanders ; foreword by Stephen King ; photographs by Jenny Bravo.
    Description: First edition. | California : Ten Speed Press, [2022] | Includes index.
    Identifiers: LCCN 2022002769 (print) | LCCN 2022002770 (ebook) |
        ISBN 9781984860026 (hardcover) | ISBN 9781984860033 (ebook)
    Subjects: LCSH: Cooking—Maine. | King, Stephen, 1947—Themes, motives. |
        Cooking in literature. | LCGFT: Literary cookbooks.
    Classification: LCC TX714 .C37315454 2022 (print) | LCC TX714 (ebook) |
        DDC 641.59741—dc23/eng/20220215
    LC record available at https://lccn.loc.gov/2022002769
    LC ebook record available at https://lccn.loc.gov/2022002770

Hardcover ISBN: 978-1-9848-6002-6
eBook ISBN: 978-1-9848-6003-3

Printed in China

Editor: Shaida Boroumand | Production Editors: Doug Ogan and Sohayla Farman
Art Director and Designer: Betsy Stromberg | Production Designers: Mari Gill and Faith Hague
Production Manager: Dan Myers | Prepress Color Manager: Jane Chinn
Food and Prop Stylist: Chantal Lambeth | Food Stylist Assistant: Sheila Jarnes
Prop Stylist Assistant: Mazie Bartels-Biswell | Photo Assistant: Linda Campos
Copyeditor: Amy Kovalski | Proofreader: Mary J. Cassells | Indexer: Elizabeth Parson
Publicist: David Hawk | Marketer: Stephanie Davis

10 9 8 7 6 5 4 3 2 1

First Edition